Gypsy Oracle Cards

Cards

A Handbook for Interpreting the Sibilla della Zingara

M. Jacqueline Murray

The information provided in this book including any tips or recommendations are meant to inspire the reader. The information provided is based on the author's experience and has been carefully considered prior to inclusion. Nevertheless, no guarantee can be granted nor is anything in this book a substitute for professional medical, psychological, legal or financial consultation. The author does not assume liability for the use or misuse of the information contained herein, nor for personal or material damage or financial losses.

The illustrations in this book are taken from the following deck of cards:
GYPSY ORACLE CARDS © Lo Scarabeo s.r.l. – Italy
ISBN 978-8883957857

Permission to use the illustrations from the cards has been given by
Lo Scarabeo s.r.l. – Italy

Editions
Print, Deluxe Edition: ISBN 978-0-9991493-0-0
Print: ISBN 978-0-9991493-1-7
E-book: ISBN 978-0-9991493-2-4

*For my husband Mike who inspires me
to take leaps beyond what I think I can
do because he is there to catch me.*

*And for my yogi, psychic, astrologer
friend Jennifer who encouraged me to
develop my psychic gifts and gave me
the Gypsy Oracle Deck that set me on
the path to writing this book. Thank you
for sharing your insights and experience
that enriched my understanding of the
cards and the service of interpreting
their meanings for others.*

*A special thank you to Puka for helping
it all come together so perfectly.*

Table of Contents

Introduction

The traditions of card reading as a means of providing answers to life's questions are centuries old. There are numerous decks to choose from for cartomancy including tarot, Lenormand, sybille or oracle style decks. The card deck discussed in this book is the Sibilla della Zingara or Gypsy Oracle Deck which is widely believed to be an evolution of a Lenormand style deck.

I write this book respectful of the traditions and origins of the cards but with a modern vision for the card meanings and interpretation. The most significant difference is that I have broadened the meanings of the cards to be more gender neutral. The traditional gender roles represented in the cards put unrealistic restraints on the readers ability to interpret today's life situations. For example, a Doctor or Scholar is not necessarily a male person as depicted on the card, but rather a person who has the attributes or plays the role of a doctor or scholar. That doesn't mean that a card never represents a male or female person in a reading, but rather it doesn't limit the interpretation to one gender or the other.

My goal in writing this book is to share my understanding of these cards and how to interpret them but I want to emphasize that the most important voice to listen to when doing a reading is your inner voice. Whether you believe that voice is divine in origin, guided by spirits, a channeling of energy or your own intuition and experience, it takes practice to tap into this source of knowledge. I don't believe the cards have magical powers, rather, they are a vehicle to tap into this source to provide insights into the situation or question being asked.

I am often asked if the cards can predict the future. I don't believe that they can because I don't believe what will happen is predetermined. The cards provide guidance; offering suggestions, warnings, encouragement, and advice. With this added insight into the situation, people and circumstances surrounding them, the inquirer can use the information to make the decisions that will shape their own future.

Card Interpretations

Each card in the Gypsy Oracle deck has it's own unique meaning. This section explains these meanings including a description of the symbolism of the card image, guidance for interpretation of the card in the straight orientation (that is when the card image is right side up) and reversed (when the card image is upside down).

Straight   Reversed

Also included are suggested interpretations of the card as it might be read in a cross spread. A description of the cross spread and other commonly used layouts are included in the Card Spread section of this book.

While researching this book, I found the original Italian title for each card. In many cases, the current title is the same, however, there are certain cards where the meaning could be interpreted quite differently if influenced by the original Italian word. For instance, the card "Despair" was previously titled "Gelosia" meaning jealousy. I have found it helpful to consider the Italian title in those cases where it broadens the card meaning as it provides an additional dimension for interpretation.

For card readers that work with different types of card decks, I have included a section correlating each card with other card systems. The fifty two Gypsy Oracle Cards can be represented by playing card with numbers (Ace, Two, Three, etc. through King) and suits (hearts, diamonds, clubs and spades). Playing card suits, known as "French suits", correspond to the Italian suits that are used for most Tarot cards (cups, coins, clubs and swords). The most similar card deck to the Gypsy Oracle Cards is the Vera Sibilla. For each card I have also included the definition of the corresponding Vera Sibilla card.

The descriptions also include numbers and dates that have been historically associated with these cards. The numbers have appeared in earlier versions of the cards but are not in the design of the current printing of this deck. For cards with numbers listed, the first number is for the card in the straight position and the second is if the card is reversed. I don't use the numbers or dates for my readings, however, others who have gifts in the areas of astrology or numerology may find insight in the numbers and dates.

Although the cards have individual meanings, the interpretation of the cards in a spread requires an understanding of how adjacent or associated cards will influence the interpretation. It would be impossible to list every possible combination but I have included examples or general guidelines for how the meaning of a single card is influenced by the others that appear in the same reading.

Cheerfulness

Original Italian title: *Allegria* meaning joy

This card is full of favorable meanings for the inquirer. The name is synonymous with joy and happiness.

- a social event, reception, wedding or baby shower, celebration
- a need to get out more and enjoy yourself, a spree
- good mood that affects all aspects of life

SYMBOLS: This card bears a drawing of a man and two women, three people, the perfect number and complete. The surroundings are opulent, the figures well dressed and refined, suggesting good fortune and wealth. The geometry of the figures forms a triangle, a symbol of divine perfection, the Trinity, which suggests hope, fertility and luck. The toast with the wine is obvious which suggests an accomplishment or event to celebrate. The wine could also indicate putting bad experiences in the past (wine symbolizing forgetfulness or neglect). It is a sign of good news, successful developments or projects, unexpected victories in every field, or moments of celebration and revelry.

STRAIGHT: The positive nature of this card is obvious. This card clearly indicates a successful event, the announcement of a favorable outcome, the goal finally reached, a challenge overcome. The mood is joyous and gratifying. The life of the inquirer is joyful. This is a serene and lively time. Relationships are harmonious. New happiness, winnings, sentimental and social stability, travel, pregnancy are all possibilities suggested by this card. In the company of negative cards, this card could be a warning that excess, lust, waste or overindulgence could lead to the unfortunate events depicted on the accompanying cards.

SUGGESTIONS FOR:
LOVE: Peace in the family, celebration of life events
WORK: Celebrating promotion, raise, compliments, good review
HEALTH: Good health or pregnancy to celebrate

ADVICE: Launch yourself into obstacles, diffuse with a laugh: joy is your trump card.

LOCATION IN A CROSS SPREAD:
- Above - Past: a past celebration or success is a contributing factor
- Below - Future: there will be something to celebrate soon
- In front - Obstacle: overcome a challenge or obstacle in order to have something to celebrate
- Behind- Advice should get out more and enjoy life, need social interaction

REVERSED: Reversed this card suggests a negative answer to the inquiry, a denied job, a failed exam, unsuccessful pregnancy, or more serious such as a wedding interrupted, broken engagement, illness or death. Joy disappears, giving way to sadness and disloyalty. There is no room for joy or happiness. Expect betrayals, lies, enemy presence, and obstacles. The inquirer feels a general malaise with deep laziness crisis, a lack of enthusiasm or loss of trust in others. Inquirer should act with caution, keep eyes open, use cunning and face a difficult situation in the short term. If in the company of many positive cards, this card could represent discomfort in social situations.

OTHER CARD SYSTEMS: Nine of Clubs
- Vera Sibilla: Nine of Clubs: Mirth: Happiness, personal realization, feeling of "finally", fertility, parties, joy

DATES: August 8 to 14

NUMBERS: 87 / 31

Child

Original Italian title: *Il Bambino*, the child

A positive card indicating new possibilities. The name is also suggestive of innocence, beginnings and creation.

- pregnancy, a baby, birth, childhood
- a new project or relationship, a fresh start, creativity
- naïve, inexperience, infancy stage or need to look after someone less able
- satisfying repressed desires and unfulfilled hopes, candor

SYMBOLS: The card bears a drawing of a baby in an ornate bassinet, clearly treasured and born into fortunate circumstances. The child's eyes are open, resting but restless. The infant represents a baby or a beginning, something being born. It suggests innocence, spontaneity, simplicity, sweetness and a hint of naivety. This image symbolizes the future and the distant future. The child also is vulnerable and needs protection indicating whatever is beginning must be nurtured and cared for in order to flourish.

STRAIGHT: The baby in the cradle, conveys the meaning of "new", the first step, the initial part of any life event personal or business. Little-by-little the seeds sown by the inquirer will grow and bear lush fruit. Creating a new life. Whatever the situation predicted by adjacent cards, it will proceed well and indicates the beginning of fortunate situations that prove advantageous. It signals the development of something very important. It can mean a pregnancy, a birth, a new love, a new friendship, a window of opportunity that will be beneficial and long lived. There is an element of surprise or an unexpected payoff. There are new possibilities, new ways to overcome daily difficulties.

SUGGESTIONS FOR:
LOVE: pregnancy, birth, beginning of a love story, fulfilling-long lasting, happy marriage.
WORK: a new job, new initiatives are successful, new ideas or creativity thrives, good choices have been made
HEALTH: childbirth, childhood ailments should not be ignored

ADVICE: Accept the new element in your life with enthusiasm and without prejudices: something is going to flourish in or near you. Approach situations with innocence, naïveté, simplicity and naturalness.

LOCATION IN A CROSS SPREAD:
- Above - Past: something new has happened or begun
- Below - Future: a new beginning or start is coming
- In front – Obstacle: will need to nurture something new
- Behind - Advice: situation requires creativity or naïveté

REVERSED: The simplest interpretation of this card reversed is that a desire for motherhood or pregnancy will not be realized. The child in this position predicts failed plans, indecisiveness, worry or anxiety resulting from a fear of losing something that has recently begun. The card reversed can also indicate there has been immaturity, imprudent or unsafe actions that could result financial losses, a series of failures in business, at work or of projects or unwise investments. The interpretation is influenced by surrounding cards. Whatever the theme of surrounding cards, something new will not be born or something small is ending and will not mature or bear fruit.

OTHER CARD SYSTEMS: Seven of Diamonds
- Vera Sibilla: Seven of Diamonds: Child: child, pets, everything that is new, beginning, inception, new situations

DATES: August 28 to September 2

NUMBERS: 47 / 1

13

Consolation

Original Italian title: *Gran Consolazione*, great consolation

This is a very positive card that predicts doubts and worries will give way to a great recovery.
- realization of desires, satisfaction, esteem, well-being and fortune
- unexpected opportunity, favorable period
- positive changes, results and events
- approval, honors

SYMBOLS: The card shows a man is sitting on a terrace with a beautiful view. He appears to be waiting for someone but does not appear anxious as he is sitting reading. He is surprised by the appearance of an angel bearing a twig and a bag of coins. The sudden consolation delivered by the angel symbolizes the unexpected gift that is freely given but has not been sought after. The twig could represent laurels suggesting unexpected recognition or honors.

STRAIGHT: A pleasant surprise is coming for the inquirer. The news is positive. The consolation is sudden and unexpected and will result in a positive outcome for the inquirer. It could be an unexpected gifts or honors, or it could be a meeting or event that results in a positive change or provides a new opportunity. A beautiful dream that has become reality. However, these rewards are deserved. They are the rewards that come to one who has believed firmly in their ideas and as a result their hopes and desires are realized.

SUGGESTIONS FOR:

LOVE: the pains of love are behind, the page has turned, relationships are enriched, new love can appear

WORK: can proceed with optimism and confidence, new initiatives take off and are rewarding

HEALTH: stress or depression gives way, worries fade, spirits are lifted, physically feel good

ADVICE: Look to the future with optimism. Be open and accepting of opportunities and changes.

LOCATION IN A CROSS SPREAD:

- Above – Past: desires and hopes have been realized
- Below – Future: a pleasant surprise is coming
- In front – Obstacle: the challenge is facing change with positivity
- Behind – Advice: hold on to your dreams, be optimistic

REVERSED: When this card is reversed it signifies missed or wasted opportunities. Literally, the failure to receive consolation so it suggests that the failure is due to forces external to the consultant, a fluke rather than a consequence. It could suggest a lack of comfort or an unexpected disappointment.

OTHER CARD SYSTEMS: Seven of Clubs

- Vera Sibilla: Seven of Clubs: Great Consolation: material well-being, stability, safety, realization, work environment, meeting

DATES: July 28 to August 1

NUMBERS: 66 / 38

Constancy

Original Italian title: *Costanza*, constancy

This is a positive card that gives assurance that with commitment, strength and determination, life's difficulties are overcome.

- continuity, steadiness, reliability, consistency, solidity
- purposeful, prudent, determined, patient
- long term, long-lasting, far-sighted
- lack of change, solid, accountability, fixed

SYMBOLS: The card depicts a woman, unruffled and secure, leaning on a ruined column. The ruined column could indicate an unwanted event that has occurred in the past but despite this, the woman is strong. Her hair is blowing in the wind but she is steadfast stubborn, perpetually wise. She is waiting for someone, prepared to fight if needed. There is a temple in the background. The temple could represent wisdom.

STRAIGHT: This card is favorable and assures the inquirer that with commitment, strength and determination they can overcome life's difficulties and achieve great things in all areas. Constancy will be rewarded. There will not be a change in attitude, commitments will be maintained, lovers will be faithful, and constancy in work will be rewarded. It might have a mild negative meaning when linked to an adverse event, suggesting that despite efforts, little or nothing will change, that the situation is unmovable or static.

SUGGESTIONS FOR:
LOVE: loyalty and sincerity are rewarded, it's a special moment for loving relationship, love will endure
WORK: time invested in work, sacrifices pay off, the image of the inquirer will improve and the future is bright
HEALTH: health is excellent, look to the future with confidence, health is protected

ADVICE: Maintain continuity with the past, be consistent and true.

LOCATION IN A CROSS SPREAD:
- Above – Past: consistency and patience has been demonstrated
- Below- Future: people or a situation will remain steadfast or constant
- In front – Obstacle: despite efforts, overcoming the status quo will be a challenge
- Behind – Advice: have a persevering and purposeful attitude

REVERSED: This card reversed indicates inconsistency, hesitation, impulsive behavior and lack of stability. It may also represent an unfair or unreliable friend. It can suggest a lack of commitment will result in dissatisfaction. In matters of love, there could be a lack of commitment, fidelity or dedication. At work, inconsistency will lead to missed opportunities. It could suggest a student has not prepared sufficiently for their exams. With respect to relationships, this card reversed can suggest there is a lack of firmness, or foundation to a relationship. Be it love or friendship, it will be fragile and one should proceed with caution.

OTHER CARD SYSTEMS: Ten of Hearts
- Vera Sibilla: Ten of Hearts: Constancy: stability, everything that lasts or is permanent, success due to dedication and sacrifice

DATES: October 15 to 20

NUMBERS: 58 / 6

Conversation

Original Italian title: *Conversazione*, conversation

This card symbolizes family reunions, and good relationships with friends and loved ones.

- dialogue, discussion, communication, being heard
- exchange of information, clarification, apologies
- weighing the pros and cons of a situation
- circle of friends

SYMBOLS: This card depicts a young woman sitting outdoors in pleasant conversation with a group of friends. She is speaking and it looks as if she is being heard because the other people appear to be interested and attentive. The conversation also appears to be a positive one. The figures all appear to be happy and content, suggesting the circumstances are positive, joy, abundance, love, renewal, or fertility.

STRAIGHT: This card is a positive one, and indicates favorable moments for the inquirer with respect to life, friendships and relationships. This card foreshadows a meeting or gathering that will take place. With this meeting, what is important is the exchange of information that conveys a point of view, an argument or advice. This card can mean a meeting between friends, a business meeting or a family gathering. This card suggests a chance for clarification, explanations or apologies. It also suggests the inquirer will be heard when they engage in conversation or discussion. Adjacent cards can suggest the nature of the meeting or who will be affected or involved. With love cards, this could suggest intimate and affectionate dialogue. Negative cards in proximity could indicate that the necessary communication may be hindered. With respect to business meetings or job interviews, this card indicates a positive outcome. It may also signal an invitation is coming or that someone wants to speak with the inquirer.

SUGGESTIONS FOR:
LOVE: announcements of birth, pregnancy, engagement, promises between lovers, family ties are strong.
WORK: inspiration, brilliant ideas for new projects are shared, important talks take place, positive job changes or promotion.
HEALTH: passing a critical phase related to health, news of pregnancy, psychological well-being, inner strength and energy

ADVICE: Communication is essential to resolve problems in any aspect of life. Do not rest until the air has been cleared.

LOCATION IN A CROSS SPREAD:
- Above – Past: conversation or meeting has taken place
- Below – Future: there will be a conversation or meeting
- In front – Obstacle: there is important information to convey or an explanation or apology is needed
- Behind - Advice open and honest communication is needed

REVERSED: When reversed this card assumes the meaning of lack of clarification, lack of communication or postponed conversations. It suggests that perhaps conversations should be avoided because the consequences may be worse than if no conversation took place. It might advise the inquirer that silence is golden and they are talking too much. If the inquiry is around love relationships, there is failure to communicate, a dispute remains unresolved, there are significant misunderstandings or there is critical information that is being withheld. In conjunction with other negative cards, it could indicate that events are stormy, desired communications do not occur, and communications fail. In conjunction with cards like Falseness or Foe, it could indicate gossip, slander, conspiracy, or other communication behind the inquirer's back that could be damaging.

OTHER CARD SYSTEMS: Ace of Hearts
- Vera Sibilla: Ace of Hearts: Conversation: words, negotiation, interview, people living with inquirer

DATES: May 21 to 27

NUMBERS: 73 / 39

19

Death

Original Italian title: *Morte*, death

This is a negative card signifying an ending.

- death, ending, divorce, time to move on
- sudden change, upheaval
- metamorphosis, transition, transcendance, rebirth

SYMBOLS: This card depicts death as a flying man, a demon with bat wings. He has a scythe over one shoulder and a skull on his hip. He looks menacingly down at the world below from a gloomy sky. The dark imagery provides contrast as death is the enemy of life. The old is bound to perish.

STRAIGHT: This card almost always means that something is coming to an end. One should not fear this card because this may not necessarily be bad news. Endings are necessary to make way for transformation; it is the natural cycle of the universe. It does suggest that something will be irreversibly lost or left behind. This could be a love, job, trip, business, career or happy time. However, this could result in something better taking its place. Faced with this card, the inquirer should consider that there is a need for a profound and radical change to take place. Although this change could be very difficult or unpleasant, it may be the necessary path to follow. Sudden painful events that lead to anguish, despair, violence, trauma or weakness are possible. This card signals the start of a stormy period but can also indicate that there will be a shift to more soothing or very positive events.

SUGGESTIONS FOR:
LOVE: the end of a marriage, relationship or engagement or the end of a bad period, revival after emotional period

WORK: a change in job or profession as likely work has become tiresome and gives little satisfaction

HEALTH: physical and emotional recovery will come after a time of illness, depression or exhaustion

ADVICE: Face the sudden change, upheaval, regret, bitterness and accept that it is over. The answer is no. Forget the past and head in another direction.

LOCATION IN A CROSS SPREAD:
- Above – Past: something has recently ended
- Below – Future: there will be a separation or ending
- In front – Obstacle: will need to deal with sudden changes, upheaval or regret
- Behind – Advice: consider that the answer is no, it's over or something has ended

REVERSED: This card reversed suggests that the situation is very negative and represents significant upheaval in the inquirer's life. Reversed this card is nefarious, shocking, unreasonable and may indicate physical death, the death of a feeling, the end of a job, business or criminal conviction. Whatever the cause, it could result in a significant disruption and a prolonged negative period. It could suggest there is an element of deceit, hatred, revenge or malicious magic. What is lost, is lost forever and could be due to deception, hidden enemies, murderers and thieves.

OTHER CARD SYSTEMS: Five of Spades
- Vera Sibilla: Five of Spades: Death: end of something or someone, fear, crisis
- Tarot: XV Death: Transition, progress, necessity, inevitability

DATES: July 15 to 20

NUMBERS: 46 / 13

Despair

Original Italian title: *Gelosia*, jealousy

This is a negative card that reveals confusion and unreasonable thoughts that result from despair, desperate jealousy, envy, loss of love and sorrow.

- being disgraced, cheated, betrayed, insulted, humiliated, dishonored, loss of face, deceived, debased, defiled, raped
- scandals, convictions, misfortunes resulting in bitterness and mistrust
- feeling sad, hopeless helpless, dejected, discouraged, shame, fear

SYMBOLS: The card depicts a man, with a gun to his head, seemingly about to commit suicide. The man's ruin seems certain should he proceed. On the table there are flowers and what seems to be a letter, suggesting the root of the problem is envy or jealousy. The pistol could indicate the urgent need to pay more attention to friends, partners or relatives who may be suffering an extreme existential crisis or self-doubt.

STRAIGHT: The meaning of this card is rooted in understanding the destructive capacity of jealousy. Jealously can lead to despair and rash and unreasonable thoughts or decisions. Jealousy of another man or woman can lead to unhealthy, dangerous even insane thoughts and lead to actions that are taken out of desperation rather than being rational. Jealousy can be related to more than love relationships. It can include envy between friends, family or business associates. In the extreme, the humiliation of the circumstances results in despair, loss of the will to live, isolation, resentment, self-pity. Although it might be flattering when a partner is jealous, it is unhealthy and can lead to destructive behaviors like excessive possessiveness, controlling, spying on email, phone calls and distrust. This card reminds the inquirer that envy among friends, colleagues and relatives can lead to unreasonable and detestable behaviors. In conjunction with other cards, it helps understand the moods of others, and the environment in which he or she is living.

SUGGESTIONS FOR:

LOVE: jealousy, fear of being betrayed, fear of not being loved makes one vulnerable, difficult times with partners

WORK: fierce competition, disagreements, hostile work environs

HEALTH: delusions, neurosis, emotional imbalance, physical and emotional stress, persecution complex

ADVICE: Be prepared for a difficult time but do not project your fears and obsessions. If it is a jealous partner, the inquirer should consider what actions or behaviors they are undertaking that could be the cause.

LOCATION IN A CROSS SPREAD:

- Above – Past: despair, doubts or jealousy have been a factor
- Below – Future: envy, jealousy, mistrust and despair are possible
- In Front – Obstacle: negative emotions, envy, sadness or unreasonable behaviors will need to be dealt with
- Behind – Advice: beware of the impact of jealousy and envy, do not act rashly

REVERSED: This card reversed suggests the moment of despair is interrupted. It doesn't mean that there is no jealousy, the card continues to indicate that it is present, but urges the consultant to consider the causes even though it has not yet caused despair. It also could signal an end to reckless or irrational behaviors other than jealousy. Confusing situations, disorder, nervousness, fatigue and falsehoods are possible at this time and it is advisable not to act impulsively or inappropriately. Rather this card urges the inquirer to continue life with courage, tackling problems possibly with the help of a loved one.

OTHER CARD SYSTEMS: Eight of Spades

- Vera Sibilla: Eight of Spades: Jealousy: financial crisis, loss of money, misfortune, darkness, dark rituals, jealousy, envy

DATES: November 2 to 7

NUMBERS: None

Doctor

Original Italian title: *Dottore*, doctor

A multipurpose card that can represent a person or a concept. It could represent an influential person, doctor, lawyer, professional, expert or wise friend or reflect the need for healing, to correct something or solve a problem.

- medicine man or woman, trusted advisor
- need for emotional or physical healing
- projects not going according to plan, bad working conditions, stress

SYMBOLS: This card shows a physician and his patient. The man seems mature, kind, sure of himself and perhaps protective. He appears to be assessing or diagnosing the patient. The serious and thoughtful expression of the doctor assisting their patient appears to reflect the concerns and question that are being asked of him. The patient appears looking up to the doctor. It suggests that the man is respected and admired and will give the patient honest and wise advice.

STRAIGHT: This card is usually positive, indicating whatever the crisis, it will be overcome. If the card represents a person, one can expect to receive an informed and assured answer. This person will provide wise advice, comfort, and authoritative guidance. The inquirer should seek advice in order to get out of or resolve the situation they are facing. The card suggests that there is a need to get out of a situation, abandon a road or get out of a period of inertia. If accompanied by other positive cards, the inquirer will encounter favorable events and people who will help, possibly unexpectedly.

SUGGESTIONS FOR:

LOVE: father, husband, grandfather, uncle who are serious, loyal reliable, sensible and genuinely will help

WORK: working relationship with leader, partner, advisor or customer is helpful and satisfactory

HEALTH: no serious problems, consult your trusted family physician or specialist for advice

ADVICE: Trust, seek advice in deciding what remedy is needed to resolve the current problem.

LOCATION IN A CROSS SPREAD:
- Above – Past: a healing or resolution has occurred with the help of a trusted advisor
- Below – Future: the situation will be resolved with the guidance of a trusted advisor
- In front – Obstacle: there is a need for healing that may require professional advice
- Behind: Advice: seek the council of a trusted advisor or professional

REVERSED: Reversed this card suggests the person we trust is of no help and may even hinder the successful resolution of the problem, disease or crisis. It may mean that the inquirer has been unprepared or unwilling to take advice or has not been making an effort to resolve the situation. The inquirer may be closed minded and refusing help. If associated with other negative cards it could mean that there will be an extended period of difficulty the inquirer will need to face alone without guidance or that there will be insufficient help available. In love, the trusted person may mislead and damage the relationship. At work, leaders or employers mislead. The reverse is almost always an indication of the cause of a situation and is a warning to re-evaluate and lay a new foundation for revival or healing.

OTHER CARD SYSTEMS: King of Clubs
- Vera Sibilla: King of Clubs: Doctor: successful influential man, doctor or graduate, the field of health or healthcare

DATES: December 11 to 20

NUMBERS: 75 / 44

Enemy

Original Italian title: *Il Nemico*, the enemy, masculine

This is a negative card describing a male enemy who is devious and will use any means to undermine one's personal or financial situation.

- opposition, forces working against, confrontation
- espionage, circumstantial evidence, distrust
- impostor, false friend, enemy
- unaware of something that is wrong or a problem arising

SYMBOLS: The card shows a man hiding behind a tree waiting for his victim. It is a lonely road, ideal for an ambush or trap. The man symbolizes a person who fights us or is plotting against us. The enemy is also a symbol of the obstacle, that separates us or prevents us from realizing a project. It is significant that it is hidden by a tree, something natural that we would not suspect would harbor something that would make us unhappy.

STRAIGHT: This card is a warning to be on guard, to weigh information and review carefully. Someone or something could be plotting against the inquirer, blocking the path forward. The associated cards help discern what activity is affected and what effect it will have on the inquirer's life. Be wary that there could be someone who is angry with us, that we have wronged and seeks revenge. This card also suggests that the enemy is unexpected, will spring seemingly from nowhere, taking the inquirer by surprise. If followed by a card indicating interruption, can indicate reconciliation, return of a friendship, end of hostilities, end of danger of obstacle.

SUGGESTIONS FOR:
LOVE: a friend or relative intrudes and disrupts a relationship or causes emotional distress

WORK: keep plans to one's self, keep good records, check contracts, expect cheating or undermining

HEALTH: agitation and tension create anxiety, heart problems or insomnia possible, burn off excess energy with sports

ADVICE: Be alert to recognize the person predicted by the card.

LOCATION IN A CROSS SPREAD:
* Above – Past: someone has undermined or blocked your progress
* Below – Future: be watchful, an enemy is lurking and will appear unexpectedly
* In front – Obstacle: someone or something is blocking progress
* Behind: Advice: be on guard, watchful as someone is working against you.

REVERSED: Reversed, this card is positive, indicating the end of an argument, hostility, or obstacle. It can also indicate a deception was a joke, a close call, or that danger was detected or an enemy disarmed before damage could be done. This card can be ambiguous if accompanied by other negative cards it could indicate a resolved problem could be re-initiated.

OTHER CARD SYSTEMS: Jack of Spades
* Vera Sibilla: Jack of Spades: Male Enemy: rival, enemy, competitor, the other man, secret, substance abuse

DATES: February 21 to March 6

NUMBERS: 78 / 27

Faithfulness

Original Italian title: *Fedelta*, fidelity

This is a positive card symbolizing loyalty, fidelity and faithfulness.

- count on support of friends, family, colleagues
- good omen, positive results
- protection,
- trust your instincts

SYMBOLS: The central image is that of a Saint Bernard near a pond or patch of snow. There is a village in the distance at the foot of mountains. Dogs are a symbol of fidelity, loyalty, sincerity, protection and instinct. In this case, the breed of dog is also significant in that it is a very large working dog that was traditionally used for alpine rescues. Thus, the card symbols suggest there are people or forces that are standing by you, willing and able to come to your aid.

STRAIGHT: This card is a good omen, and suggests that the inquirer can trust those close to them and count on the help of others. Fidelity of lovers is a fundamental interpretation of this card, however, it also characterizes other relationships or situations, depending on the circumstances and associated cards. If the associated cards indicate the birth of a love relationship, friendship or business association, it suggests that this relationship will be founded on a solid foundation of trust and loyalty. This card can signify a solid working relationship, a faithful partner, a loyal and sincere friend, a loving and faithful lover, or a faithful husband, wife, boyfriend or girlfriend. The card can also indicate feelings of faithfulness, loyalty or trust. The inquirer has the security and support that leads to happiness, abundance, recognition, love and esteem. Negative cards that indicate an interruption or break could indicate that there will be an interruption or end to that which is faithful.

SUGGESTIONS FOR:

LOVE: partners are loyal and trustworthy, disagreements will be swept away by their faithfulness

WORK: teamwork gives desired results, everyone will be rewarded, all will benefit through professional relationships

HEALTH: any malaise is trivial, a little pampering and affection from close family or friends is the cure

ADVICE: Be faithful and accepting of the loyalty and faithfulness of those who love and care for you.

LOCATION IN A CROSS SPREAD:
- Above – Past: others have been faithful and loyal
- Below – Future: there will be a positive outcome due to support of others
- In front – Obstacle: you may need to be rescued, supported by others
- Behind: Advice: trust those close to you to be faithful and protective

REVERSED: The most likely interpretation of the reverse of this card is the simplest, that there is infidelity, disloyalty, betrayal or misplaced trust, a breach of duty or a responsibility ignored. It suggests that there has been a change in a relationship for the worse, or there is a potential for that change if unfaithful, irresponsible or unethical actions are taken.

OTHER CARD SYSTEMS: Nine of Hearts
- Vera Sibilla: Nine of Hearts: Faithfulness: feelings of love, trustworthiness, everything according to plan, everything according to its nature

DATES: August 8 to 14

NUMBERS: 88 / 37

Falseness

Original Italian title: *Falsita*, falsehood

This negative card suggests the need to be careful and watchful, flattery conceals cheating and falsehoods.

- betrayal, deception of the worst kind, lies, corruption, defensiveness.
- something or someone fake, two-faced person
- something wrong, negative
- trying to cover up a mistake or lie, lying to yourself

SYMBOLS: This card shows a beautiful domestic cat, sitting on a red pillow. Cats are a symbol of gossip, rumors, and untruths. The red pillow symbolizes jealousy and envy. The cat also has claws, with the ability to scratch or pounce unexpectedly when it appears to be quietly resting. The ability to ambush their prey, possibly leaving scratches that are painful and long-lasting. The deception of the soothing purr that disguises a nature that can transform to scratch or injure without warning.

STRAIGHT: This card is a warning to be aware that things may not be as they seem on the surface. This card can symbolize a person who is "false", that is, not genuine or sincere. Be cautious, the inquirer could encounter meanness and wickedness, the lure of false flattery or double dealing. This card can also help interpret a situation. If associated cards relate to communication, meetings, or partnerships, this card suggests empty promises, weak foundations, insincerity, or deception. In love relationships, this card strongly suggests that the partner's heart is not entirely sincere, that there may be lies and the inquirer could be hurt unexpectedly. Be aware that this card can also point to the inquirer, that their behavior is "false" in some way.

SUGGESTIONS FOR:
> LOVE: the partner is not entirely sincere, new relationship not meant to last, lies and opportunism amongst family and friends
> WORK: all that glitters is not gold, weigh options carefully, a mistake could be costly
> HEALTH: better recheck results, something is not right

ADVICE: Proceed with caution with people and situations, anticipate that things are not as they appear.

LOCATION IN A CROSS SPREAD:
- Above – Past: things have not been as they seem, a falsehood has been discovered
- Below – Future: you will encounter falsehood in a person or situation
- In front – Obstacle: insincerity, gossip, or false information poses a challenge
- Behind: Advice: anticipate that things are not as they appear

REVERSED: This card reversed indicates the end of a period of falsehood, that the truth will come out, secrets are revealed, and deceptions are uncovered. Insincere behaviors, gossip, slander, jealousy and envy will cease to be a factor. It may give an answer to the inquirer's question, indicating there has been no deceit.
In the company of other cards, that are negative, the reverse could suggest that things are worse than anticipated, betrayals, extramarital affairs, or infidelity of partners, employees, family and friends.

OTHER CARD SYSTEMS: Four of Diamonds
- Vera Sibilla: Four of Diamonds: Falsehood: insincerity, lie, distortion of reality, illusion, deception

DATES: May 8 to 14

NUMBERS: 80 / 16

Foe

Original Italian title: *Nemica*, enemy, feminine

This is a negative card that either represents a female that is wicked or a backstabber, or an event that is a hindrance.
- female enemy, rival, competition, fake friend
- wickedness, hypocrisy, bad advice
- intrigues, deceit, fraud

SYMBOLS: The card depicts a woman on the threshold of an open door. She represents a rival in love, work or family. She could be a lover, wife, jealous girlfriend, or greedy woman or any other type of rival. The door is open, suggesting that she can freely enter. It is unclear if she has been invited or if the door was left open by accident. There is still the possibility of keeping this person at bay as the door could be closed before she enters.

STRAIGHT: This card signals that there is a person or event that will interfere in the inquirers life. If it represents a person, it is one who sees the inquirer as a foe or target. Unlike the Enemy card, the Foe represents someone who is out in the open, known and visible to the inquirer, although, it may be someone dear that they do not suspect. It could represent a friend who is insincere and not to be trusted. Bad advice or gossip that damages the projects or ambitions of the inquirer is also possible. This card can also represent immorality or infidelity. The positive aspect of this card is that there is still time to avoid the damage, the inquirer need only recognize the threat and close the door.

SUGGESTIONS FOR:
LOVE: a rival, could be separated or divorced, wants to break up relationship, should be kept at a distance
WORK: dishonest person who disrupts work, office gossip
HEALTH: can reveal possibility of disease, if multiple cards suggest issues, repeat or duplicate tests recommended

ADVICE: Defend yourself, close the door to the threat. It is best to keep this person away, do not accept advice, do not confide joys nor sorrows.

LOCATION IN A CROSS SPREAD:
- Above – Past: a foe or rival has caused this situation
- Below – Future: there will be interfering forces impacting the situation
- In front – Obstacle: there will be a challenge from a female rival or competition
- Behind: Advice: look for the foe and take steps to keep them out of your life

REVERSED: If associated with negative cards the reverse could indicate that the danger is imminent. It could indicate that the inquirer already has a love rival, dangerous person, whisperer, gossiper doing damage in their life who has no intention of stopping. Only if associated with very positive cards, could it suggest that a dispute, hazard, obstacle or enemy has been removed.

OTHER CARD SYSTEMS: Queen of Spades
- Vera Sibilla: Queen of Spades: Female Enemy: rival, competitor, the other woman, secrets, substance abuse

DATES: March 7 to 13

NUMBERS: 65 / 41

Fortune

Original Italian title: *Fortuna*, luck

This is a very positive card symbolizing luck and good fortune.

- lucky streak, dreams come true, victorious
- happy at work, positive business transactions, change for the better
- inner riches, discover hidden talents

SYMBOLS: Fortune is depicted as a blindfolded woman holding a cornucopia and distributing gold coins and money. The blindfold obscures where she is precisely looking although she is looking up towards the heavens. Traditional depictions of luck show her blindfolded to suggest that she does not see who is benefiting, leaving open the possibility that it could be anyone.

STRAIGHT: This card indicates that whatever the inquiry, fate will deliver a positive outcome with regards to wealth or well-being. The hopes of the inquirer will be realized. It suggests that a fortuitous circumstance or chance event will bring an emotional or monetary windfall. This card is one that "lights" associated cards suggesting a lucky and positive resolution of the situation. This card weakens negative cards such as those that indicate failure, death or an ending. It suggests interruption of those negative situations and fate will intervene on the behalf of the inquirer to deliver the beginning of a successful period, new love, win, job, or fortunate circumstance that will be favorable to the inquirer. Unexpected kindness, unearned wealth, maturity, health, and security are all gifts fate can deliver. It also could indicate the arrival of a sudden inheritance, a win or chance meeting. Although determination and will to succeed remains the responsibility of the inquirer, success is near. If the situation involves a big problem to be solved, the inquirer can look forward to resolution and a brighter future.

SUGGESTIONS FOR:
LOVE: an important meeting will take place, serenity or reconciliation between lovers, meetings with trusted friends, relatives
WORK: career advancement or promotion, a big win or sale, successful launch, large inheritance
HEALTH: positive clinical results, pregnancy, psychological well-being, physical and sexual energy high, satisfaction

ADVICE: Believe your dreams will come true and dare to attract good fortune.

LOCATION IN CROSS SPREAD:
- Above – Past: has recently had a lucky period or event
- Below – Future: look forward to a fortunate event, emotional or financial win
- In front – Obstacle: change could come quickly as a result of abundance, triumph or success
- Behind: Advice: believe in yourself and move forward confident in a positive outcome

REVERSED: When reversed, luck is not on the inquirer's side. There is a need to act prudently and decisively to address the situation. When the query pertains to a relationship, the reverse suggests a slowdown or betrayal. In work situations, it suggests inexperience, slow progress and losses. The associated cards will determine the if this card indicates a singular event or a period of time. It could represent the loss of the game, a challenging business period, a lack of competitive advantage, a lover's rejection or rejection of an application for a job. When associated with positive cards it indicates that the inquirer must transit a short negative period before realizing a positive outcome or that success will come very gradually.

OTHER CARD SYSTEMS:
- Vera Sibilla: Five of Clubs: Fortuna: good luck, success outside inquirer's control

DATES: April 15 to 20

NUMBERS: 59 / 5

Friend

Original Italian title: *Amica,* friend, feminine

This positive card represents a trustworthy and loyal female figure.

- friendship, trust, security, faithfulness
- help, attentiveness, good advice
- positive news, gifts,
- your own best friend

SYMBOLS: The card shows an elegant young woman carrying a bunch of flowers. The flowers symbolize a gift, just as friendship is a treasured gift. The woman is coming forward with a kind expression suggesting she is offering help, comfort, advice or gifts. The woman appears to be in a house or home suggesting that this is a familiar, close personal friend.

STRAIGHT: This card suggests the presence of a friend, someone who will provide friendship, aid or bring good cheer. The friend may be a counselor, someone who provides support and valuable guidance after listening to our problems. This person may also be a confidante, one who keeps secrets faithfully and is sincere and trustworthy. It also suggests that the inquirer should feel confident, either in persons close to them or in a situation. This card reassures that the environment will be pleasant, cozy, and free of hostility and there will be people who happily join the company of the inquirer. This card is also an announcement that there will be favorable circumstances, situations or events, sometimes unexpectedly so. Depending on the accompanying cards, this card could be interpreted as a journey, outing or meeting taking place with a group of friends. In some cases, this card points back to the inquirer, suggesting that they need to be their own best friend, be kind and generous with themselves or need to be a friend to others.

SUGGESTIONS FOR:

LOVE: signals that an important meeting will take place, other cards will be needed to determine the fate of the relationship

WORK: meetings will take place in a comfortable setting or atmosphere

HEALTH: the inquirer may need to encourage a friend to seek help from a physician

ADVICE: Friendship is both giving and receiving; learn to trust accept the gifts of friendship

LOCATION IN CROSS SPREAD:
- Above – Past: a friend has played a significant role
- Below – Future: a friend will be supportive and true
- In front – Obstacle: having confidence in a friend for advice, accepting council and support
- Behind: Advice: be open to give and receive the gifts of friendship

REVERSED: The most likely reversed interpretation is to suggest a problem with a relationship with a friend. This could be the presence of an unfaithful friend, someone who can't keep a secret, or highlight a misunderstanding or argument with someone close to the inquirer. The environment is unfavorable, uncertain and the inquirer may feel isolated. It could also be an indication that the inquirer does not seek out friendships, does not confide in others, is difficult to get along with or will need to face difficulties alone. This card in conjunction with the "Enemy" card could indicate that a friend will become a foe or false friend that could do more harm than an unfamiliar enemy.

OTHER CARD SYSTEMS: Four of Clubs
- Vera Sibilla: Four of Clubs: Friend: confidante, guest, relationship of trust

DATES: April 9 to 14

NUMBERS: 89 / 25

Frivolity

Original Italian title: *Leggerezza*, lightness

A descriptive card symbolizing lightness, superficiality, inconsistency or carefree joy.
- undecided, fickle, irregular, changing
- impulsive, thoughtless, perilous behavior

SYMBOLS: A butterfly is the main image on this card. Butterflies are delicate and a symbol of lightheartedness and joy. They can also symbolize hope, resurrection, immortality and the souls of the dead. The behavior of a butterfly is also significant, lightly jumping from flower to flower suggesting superficiality, fickleness, and irresponsibility. The insect's wings suggest mobility and restlessness, or looking for something better. The butterfly has landed on an isolated branch and flower. The single flower pictured suggests that the butterfly is also solitary.

STRAIGHT: This card is generally positive in that is suggests lightness and a care-free existence. However, frivolity is a superficial behavior, often irresponsible, and can indicate one who jumps from one thing to another, underestimating the gravity of events. Superficiality, undervaluing people or situations, or disregard for the details are also characteristics communicated with this card. This card warns of perilous behavior that could result in later regrets or saying or doing things without considering the consequences. It can also suggest that the inquirer is one who is perched close to the edge, content to be in precarious balance. The meaning of this card is not decisive, rather it is descriptive of a mood or feeling and does not strongly influence associated cards. This card can signify a person who is scatterbrained or flighty or a state of dizziness or confusion.

SUGGESTIONS FOR:
LOVE: perhaps a moment of uncertainty with lovers or relatives, don't do something rash you might regret
WORK: do not make decisions hastily or randomly, put off important decisions until you can make them thoughtfully
HEALTH: think positively, maybe take a break, get away and don't take life so seriously

ADVICE: Do not take yourself too seriously, but recognize that superficial or frivolous behavior can have consequences.

LOCATION IN CROSS SPREAD:
- Above – Past: recently, things have been light and carefree
- Below – Future: people or situations that are carefree or frivolous are on the horizon
- In front – Obstacle: being scatterbrained, flighty or indecisive will be the challenge
- Behind: Advice: avoid superficial or thoughtless behavior

REVERSED: This card is considered positive when it appears reversed. It could spell the end of superficial or irresponsible behavior. It takes on a negative meaning only if it signals the end of a carefree time.   This card is strongly influenced by other cards. If associated cards suggest a past painful event, reversed this card suggests it will be some time before cares will be lifted. If associated with negative and relationship cards, it could indicate the inability to maintain commitments, betrayal, infidelity or disloyalty.

OTHER CARD SYSTEMS: Ten of Clubs
- Vera Sibilla: Ten of Clubs: Levity: reduces good and bad of associated cards, inconsistency, imprudence, lack of attention or foresight

DATES: August 15 to 20

NUMBERS: 50 / 15

Gift

Original Italian title: *Omaggio di Preziosi*, tribute of precious items, valuables

This is generally a good omen card suggesting the realization of aspirations or wishes, or the arrival of a gift or inheritance.

- winnings, inheritance, abundance
- situation improves, successful endeavor, achievement
- bribery, flattery

SYMBOLS: The room depicted is quite empty except for a table on which there is a box containing precious stones (gemstones) and a winged statue. The room itself looks elegant with gold trim, a painting and red drapes. The precious stones represent a gift either financial, such as an inheritance or winnings, or situational, like a brilliantly passed exam or improvement in the workplace. The emptiness of the room can indicate there is a void; that material things alone do not fill spiritual and emotional needs. The box symbolizes a home for our most precious, intimate and secret thoughts and feelings, be they conscious or unconscious, on display or hidden inside. The table pictured has many legs suggesting that the weight of the riches requires extra support.

STRAIGHT: This card suggests a situation that suddenly and dramatically improves. This could be due to an uncertain period coming to an end or that considerable help has been given that changes the situation for the better. It can represent overcoming obstacles which give way to success and esteem. Although usually considered a positive card, this card can be ambiguous in that material wealth can distract or dazzle and result in vanity, greed or be detrimental to relationships. There is a responsibility that comes with weath. When this card is associated with "Falseness" or other negative cards, it could indicate flattery, false devotion, bribes or deception. It can also indicate a situation where someone is trying to buy affection or favor.

SUGGESTIONS FOR:
LOVE: gifts exchanged between lovers, happiness within reach, union has social, economic or emotional benefits
WORK: many projects come to fruition, markets move in a positive direction, professional success and improved image
HEALTH: therapies and cures are successful, results are as desired, all will be well soon

ADVICE: Accept gifts graciously but be wary of the motivations of the giver. Check for strings attached. Be aware of the responsibility.

LOCATION IN CROSS SPREAD:
- Above – Past: personal situation has recently dramatically improved
- Below – Future: the situation will dramatically improve, abundance and aspirations or dreams will be realized
- In front – Obstacle: rewards to be gained if obstacles are overcome, be aware of the burden of wealth and privilege
- Behind: Advice: be cautious of the source of gifts or compliments and the weight that comes with great fortune

REVERSED: When reversed this card represents a loss of some kind. This could be a gift not received, a lost inheritance or other unexpected loss or debt. It can represent the inability to save money, to not set aside what's necessary or to squander money. It could represent finance and stock market losses, the sale of items to procure money or bad investments. If accompanied by the "Thief" card it can indicated a theft, scam or blackmail. This card is only positive when reversed if it is associated with cards suggesting victory, success or achievement which could indicate the end of a period of economic dependence or blackmail.

OTHER CARD SYSTEMS: Three of Diamonds
- Vera Sibilla: Eight of Diamonds: Present of Jewels: Objects, proposal, offer, luxury, everything right or luxurious, parcel

DATES: September 2 to 7

NUMBERS: None

Haughtiness

Original Italian title: *La Superbia*, pride

This is a card that communicates an attitude of superiority, pride, or lack of humility
- arrogance, conceit, vanity, showing off
- overly ambitious

SYMBOLS: The central figure of this card is a peacock, with its beautiful fan tail. The peacock is characterized as an animal that likes to celebrate their plumage, displaying it proudly and symbolizes a person who is full of themselves, lust or vanity. This peacock is not displaying his plumage, rather is calm and settled and sure of his position. This peacock is perched on a dry branch, devoid of leaves, this barrenness symbolizes losing sight of what is important while admiring one's self. In the background, there is a wall which symbolizes the isolation and barriers that come from an excess of pride.

STRAIGHT: This card describes a person, situation or behavior that is influenced by an excess of pride or lack of humility. It indicates an unbalanced attitude, perceiving one's self or a situation in an overly positive light. This card can suggest a situation where the lack of humility can damage the inquirer such as the inability to acknowledge one's mistakes or limitations. It is a warning against being charmed by pride such that the inquirer is blinded to their surroundings, the reality of a situation or the inner qualities of people around them. An excess of pride can result in contempt for others and detachment. It is a card to remind us that when we are treated, or treat others with haughtiness, coldness or detachment, we cut ourselves off and cultivate an atmosphere where misunderstanding, hatred or despair can develop. If this card is associated with many positive cards, it can indicate something to be proud of, an achievement or success is near at hand. A healthy ego is good, but do not become excessively proud.

SUGGESTIONS FOR:

LOVE: the inquirer enjoys the admiration of many suitors, new loves are favorable, pride can cause relationships to fail

WORK: the inquirer's skill and ability will be noticed, successful interview or new job is possible

HEALTH: energy and well-being are not lacking, physical health is good.

ADVICE: A healthy ego is a good thing, but be mindful of your behavior, exercise greater humility.

LOCATION IN CROSS SPREAD:
- Above – Past: an excess of pride, arrogance or conceit has led to this situation
- Below – Future: a major achievement or success is possible
- In front – Obstacle: an excess of pride can lead to isolation, misunderstandings
- Behind: Advice: acknowledge strengths and limitations, avoid haughtiness

REVERSED: When reversed this card suggests a healthy awareness of one's limitations as well as their strengths. It may indicate the need to be more sure of one's self and be proud. With this balance, relationships can be restored as there is demolition of the walls that separate. It can indicate the resumption of a friendship or relationship, or an improvement in relationships with colleagues or friends. This card does not influence surrounding cards, it indicates a past behavior that has been resolved. It can be a negative card if it is associated with reversed cards such that the combination suggests sadness or emotional turbulence.

OTHER CARD SYSTEMS: Two of Clubs
- Vera Sibilla: Two of Clubs: Pride: amulet for improvement, beauty, magic

DATES: March 28 to April 2.

NUMBERS: 69 / 18

Hope

Original Italian title: *Speranza*, hope

This is a positive card, providing encouragement that relief for the current situation is coming.

- anticipation, waiting
- believing in a positive outcome
- clairvoyance, psychic powers, translation

SYMBOLS: The card depicts a troubled woman. The setting is an open space with a beautiful sky and she is sitting alone on a hill or a rock. She is bending in on herself, curled almost into a fetal position. Her position suggests she is focused within herself and that the impact of her hopes is very personal. She has a white blindfold and is holding on to a frame with a chain. The blindfold suggests an inability to see outward, so she is focused inward. Hopes come from within. They are born from introspection and clairvoyance.

STRAIGHT: This card is a positive one that suggests that events will turn in favor of the inquirer. Whatever situation the inquirer has been focused on, it will be resolved. It is not only realizing the hopes and desires of the heart but having confidence that the situation will be favorably resolved. This card can be more than just an answer to a question, it can help elucidate deeper meaning for other associated cards. With ending cards, hope could be extinguished signaling a time to give up or move on. It can symbolize past hopes, past beliefs or certainties that must be abandoned in order to move forward. It can suggest we need to build new hopes for the future, to look inward and understand what are our deepest desires and acknowledge them.

SUGGESTIONS FOR:
LOVE: previous disappointments will resolve, despite appearances, what has been lost will be regained, maintain hope
WORK: although the situation is critical, there is reason for optimism, a strategy executed will be successful
HEALTH: will power and courage are reinforced, adverse medical conditions will be overcome

ADVICE: Believe in your hopes and vision for the future.

LOCATION IN CROSS SPREAD:
- Above – Past: something hoped for has recently materialized, deep desires have been realized
- Below – Future: there is hope that the situation will resolve favorably
- In front – Obstacle: recognizing the difference between what can be hoped for and what is hopeless
- Behind: Advice: maintain your focus, look inside yourself for your vision for the future

REVERSED: This card reversed suggests plans for the future will be disrupted. This card warns that the inquirer has misplaced hopes, for whatever situation they have been "hoping" to unfold. Enthusiasm will be dampened, or expectations will be dashed. It represents a pessimistic mood or discontent with the way a situation unfolds. Only when associated with rival or enemy cards, could this card take on a positive message of ending the hopes of others to take advantage or defeat us.

OTHER CARD SYSTEMS: Eight of Hearts
- Vera Sibilla: Eight of Hearts: Hope: realization of hope, success, investment, meeting, solution of problems

DATES: October 2 to 7

NUMBERS: 77 / 8

House

Original Italian title: *Casa*, house

This positive card can symbolize either a physical place, a home or personal epicenter or an emotion of security, solidity and prosperity.

- family and emotional bonds
- home, office, security
- responsibilities, self-reliance, independence

SYMBOLS: The card depicts a large and well maintained house. The house is a symbol of comfort, stability, security, protection and family. The house is not just a building or family residence, it is the central place through which life and love flow. The house as a home is the place where the family gathers and represents the origins of the family; it's roots or foundation.

STRAIGHT: This card suggests a stable environment. It can represent more than a family situation, it can also represent a stable work environment, or relationship. The card also suggests serenity in the home and family harmony. When interpreted in the context of other cards, it can represent the essence or heart of the problem or situation.

SUGGESTIONS FOR:

LOVE: love relationships are sweet, passionate and fulfilling, new relationships are stable, reconciliation can occur

WORK: economic stability, success, sales and new deals are as expected

HEALTH: good health, strength and mind is relaxed and free of stress

ADVICE: Feel secure in your surroundings, stability, protection and help is near.

LOCATION IN CROSS SPREAD:
- Above – Past: you have depended on your home for stability and protection
- Below – Future: stability and protection is in your future
- In front – Obstacle: stability and roots are needed to overcome this situation
- Behind: Advice: trust in the stability of your surroundings.

REVERSED: This card is very negative when reversed. It symbolizes breakdowns in family relationships, quarrels, misunderstandings, or broken dreams. When the inquirer asks regarding a loved one, reversed this card signifies breakups, broken engagements, divorce, or dissolved partnerships. It is a warning to take stock of relationships, be they at home, in the office or with friends. It can also signal the end of a business relationship or failure of an enterprise.

OTHER CARD SYSTEMS: Two of Hearts
- Vera Sibilla: Two of Hearts: House: building, house, real estate, the core of the issue, domestic environment

DATES: May 2 to June 2

NUMBERS: 62 / 22

Journey

Original Italian title: *Viaggio*, travel, trip

This is a positive card that signifies travel or mobility.

- trip, vacation
- relocation, moving
- agility, evolution, change
- going forward, making progress, evolution of a situation

SYMBOLS: The central figure of this card is a well-dressed man on a fine horse. He is carrying a pack and blanket with him, suggesting he is prepared for a long journey. The horse symbolizes our emotions and talents, harnessed and directed to move us forward be it towards success, communication or a destination. The traveler is on a path or road, that extends behind and ahead. Although it is unclear how long it is, it suggests that the journey has begun, symbolizing that everything that has been previously done or experienced has led to this moment in time.

STRAIGHT: This card suggests a positive change for the inquirer. The most literal meaning is a change in location, travel for business or pleasure or someone coming or going. Long distance travel is likely rather than short trips. It can also represent change in a situation; one that it is evolving, moving forward or resolving. Whichever the case, it suggests that things are moving for or around the inquirer. It can also suggest to the inquirer that they need to abandon the old and move on to something new. In some cases, it is a suggestion that the inquirer plan a trip or travel. Although mostly a positive card, it can take on a negative meaning of saying goodbye to someone or something going away. Associated with the "House" card it could indicate a change of residence or with "Room" a visit to a hotel or rental accommodation. Associated with the "Letter" it could represent travel documents or passport.

SUGGESTIONS FOR:
LOVE: a holiday or travel with loved one, honeymoon, a new relationship as a result of travel
WORK: a career involving travel, a driver, pilot, seaman, a transfer or relocation for work or business trip
HEALTH: travel may be required to seek out a specialist or therapy

ADVICE: Life is a continual evolution; keep moving. Staying still can result in missed opportunities.

LOCATION IN CROSS SPREAD:
- Above – Past: there has been a change in location or direction that has affected this situation
- Below – Future: a situation will make progress or travel will occur
- In front – Obstacle: the challenge will be a change in location or long distance travel
- Behind: Advice: moving forward, or changing location is suggested

REVERSED: This card reversed suggests the failure of a trip, a canceled vacation, a journey to be avoided, a missed appointment, or something or someone is late or does not arrive. It suggests a lack of momentum. It can also suggest a reluctance to meet new people or visit new places. If associated with relationship cards, it could signal the relationship has ceased to move forward or has taken a step backwards. If associated with work and business, it could be a project that is stagnant or a promotion or transfer will not occur.

OTHER CARD SYSTEMS: Three of Clubs
- Vera Sibilla: Three of Clubs: Journey: travel, change, movement, change of place / project

DATES: April 3 to 8

NUMBERS: 54 / 23

Joyfulness

Original Italian title: *Allegrezza al Cuore*, joyous heart

This is a very positive card signifying joy, lightheartedness and merriment.

- glee, gaiety, joyous time
- pleasure from entertainment or creativity
- satisfaction, relief, resolution, celebration, achievements, promotions

SYMBOLS: This card shows two girls and a boy in a spontaneous dance in a garden. Their youth suggests energy and joyful exuberance. Their clothing colors suggest hope (green), friendship or innocence (white) and love (red). There is a column or monument covered in red roses in the background. Red roses often symbolize love or matters of the heart. The number of figures, three, suggests the perfection of this moment.

STRAIGHT: This card signals a period of joy and happiness for the inquirer. It assures the inquirer that their wishes will be satisfied and whatever they are hoping for will come to pass. It predicts a favorable time when work, home, relationships or investments bring satisfaction and pleasure. This card suggests that the inquirer will have the strength and resources to successfully achieve their goal or happiness. In the presence of negative or ending cards, this card could indicate that a carefree period is coming to an end.

SUGGESTIONS FOR:
  LOVE: the effort has paid off, relationship will be joyful, new encounters are born under a lucky star, happiness for the couple
  WORK: celebrate a promotion, success at work, bonus, increase in pay, rewards are at hand for work or school
  HEALTH: take a break, from now on all is resolved, no problems

ADVICE: Accept with gratitude the gifts of destiny – be they great or small.

LOCATION IN CROSS SPREAD:
- Above – Past: there has recently been a reason for joyfulness
- Below – Future: the situation will come to a successful and happy resolution
- In front – Obstacle: allow yourself to be happy and enjoy
- Behind: Advice: be grateful and enjoy all you have received or achieved

REVERSED: This card reversed is simply the opposite, it indicates a real disappointment. It suggests the heart will be restless, there could be a lack of ideas, lack of initiative, lack of peace or the inability to live life to its fullest. It can be a warning that a difficult time is coming when there will be doubt and uncertainty. The times ahead may be sad or there may be disappointments, broken friendships, or financial challenges. When it is a work situation, it could indicate concern; in family relationships, disagreement and lack of harmony. In academic or economic situations, it could indicate anxiety and goals not achieved. Only in the case where this card reversed is associated with an "interruption" card does it signify the end of a "dark" period and coming happiness.

OTHER CARD SYSTEMS: Five of Hearts
- Vera Sibilla: Five of Hearts: Joy in the Heart: quick and positive results, engagement, job, family

DATES: June 15 to 20

NUMBERS: 83 / 42

Letter

Original Italian title: *Lettera*, letter

This is a neutral card signifying communication, news or information that could be either positive or negative.

- a message, letter, note, email, text message
- an answer, approval, contract or document
- a new opportunity or challenge

SYMBOLS: This card shows a hand holding a letter. We only see the hand, thus the messenger is unknown, however, the hand and clothes suggest that the messenger is male. The representation is impersonal or mysterious. The setting in the background is that of a home, and the letter itself is addressed to someone specific suggesting that the letter will come directly and will have a personal impact.

STRAIGHT: This card specifically refers to information that comes in written form such as a letter or email. This type of communication could contain a wide variety of messages. It could express feelings, request a meeting, protest something, request an answer, or give an apology or explanation. It is not generic news, it is a document from a specific sender to the recipient. The anonymity of the bearer also indicates that it can either be a missive for the inquirer or from the inquirer and it could be delivered by a postman, courier, family member, friend or an official like a baliff or in an electronic form. What is most important is is the content of this communication so it is essential to consider associated cards for the subject matter and whether or not it will be positive or negative.

SUGGESTIONS FOR:
LOVE: communication between friends, lovers, spouses or relatives
WORK: contract negotiations, mediation or school exams
HEALTH: medical reports or results, linguistic or psychology sessions

ADVICE: Be mindful that with information there is often a decision to be made, take time to consider your choices.

LOCATION IN CROSS SPREAD:
- Above – Past: written communication has recently been received
- Below – Future: a message or letter will arrive or be sent very soon
- In front – Obstacle: a document or message is needed to move the situation forward
- Behind: Advice: consider what communication needs to occur and who must initiate it

REVERSED: When reversed this card suggests that a letter or document will not come or will be late. It could be a loved one who does not write when they said, a confirmation that doesn't come, or an invitation not being extended. Reversal does not suggest either bad new or good news – just that it will not arrive as expected. For example, if the inquirer is expecting bad news, it suggests that it wil not come. It also might indicate that the inquirer has failed to reach out and someone is waiting for them to write.

OTHER CARD SYSTEMS: Two of Diamonds
- Vera Sibilla: Two of Diamonds: Letter: written communication, paper, document

DATES: April 28 to May 2

NUMBERS: 58 / 2

Lord

Original Italian title: *Gran Signore*, great lord

This is a positive card symbolizing nobility, good will, generosity, strength and reason or a person of privilege or authority.

- protection, supervision, guidance, advice
- gentleman, employer, boss
- nobility, wealth, status
- educated, responsible, sensitive, passionate

SYMBOLS: The central figure of this card is an elegantly dressed man. His attire, elaborate hat, long well-groomed hair and mustache all suggest he is a noble man. He is leading a horse and is wearing riding boots and gloves suggesting he has just paused in his ride. He has both a walking stick and a sword, suggesting he is grounded but prepared to defend and protect if necessary. He is looking out from the card, with a benevolent look, suggesting he is attentive to the inquirer.

STRAIGHT: This card can represent a person, a 20 to 40 year old man, who is successful, noble, well-meaning, kind, polite, not intimidating, and friendly. This person can be trusted to guide, advise and protect. It is a positive card, suggesting a happy moment, feelings of success, achievement and fulfillment. When associated with love cards, it could represent a man who is destined for the inquirer. It could also represent the employer, boss, or other professional important to the inquirer. It can suggest an encounter with this person, a perfect man, ready to give of himself to protect or bring love. It can also represent a situation, one that is right, a positive environment, where the inquirer is surrounded by kindness and good people. The nobility could be one of action, a kind gesture or good intention.

SUGGESTIONS FOR:

LOVE: a man you are lucky to have, nice, admired, serious and faithful, can't help falling in love with a man like this

WORK: proven professional, prepared, capable, far-sighted, successful, prepared with a special touch

HEALTH: in good shape, healthy, energetic, can perform at work or sports, vitality

ADVICE: Avail yourself of another's strength, generosity and knowledge. Trust their guidance and support.

LOCATION IN CROSS SPREAD:

- Above – Past: you have had the support of a good person
- Below – Future: a reliable, strong person will play a role
- In front – Obstacle: the challenge will be to accept love, help, protection, or guidance.
- Behind: Advice: trust in a good and noble person for support and guidance

REVERSED: When this card appears reversed it suggests a man of poor character; a husband who doesn't love, a selfish employer, or an irresponsible professional. A fallen man, shameless, without scruples, who is in poor shape either emotionally or physically. This can suggest a man who has been wounded by life. This card warns of deception and danger that could come from a man of undesirable character.

OTHER CARD SYSTEMS: Kind of Hearts
- Vera Sibilla: King of Hearts: Great Lord: mature man, sugar daddy, boss, married woman's husband

DATES: February 11 to 20

NUMBERS: 55/ 24

Love

Original Italian title: *Amore*, love

This is a positive card symbolizing love and eroticism.

- new love is born, happy in love
- affection, intense feelings, romance, sensuality

SYMBOLS: The card depicts a chubby reclining angel, Cupid, his bow and quiver of arrows at the ready. There are a pair of white doves above him, flying free, playful and happy, symbolizing a love that has been born and is flying to the highest highs. Both Cupid and the doves have wings, suggesting that love should be given wings and allowed to take flight. At the base of the column where Cupid rests, there are red roses representing the blossoming of love and the scent of sensuality.

STRAIGHT: This card is a very positive omen for the love life of the inquirer. There are no impediments to love, in fact, Cupid's arrow will strike and a new love will bloom or love has already been born and will reach new heights. It suggests there is a mutual love, with deep affection, sexual compatibility, and one that will result in joy and happiness. For existing lovers, it is an invitation to awaken your love, strive to improve it and make it better.

SUGGESTIONS FOR:

LOVE: stability or recovery of a loving relationship, passionate relationships family happiness, new love

WORK: good omen for family owned businesses, excellent potential for earnings or investments, the path forward is clear

HEALTH: good health and happiness, extra energy, nothing can stop the inquirer

ADVICE: Love and happiness is within your reach, recognize and grab it now.

LOCATION IN CROSS SPREAD:

- Above – Past: true love has been a significant supporting factor
- Below – Future: there will be true love or a new love soon
- In front – Obstacle: recognize love and have a loving attitude
- Behind: Advice: take time to let love bloom and grow

REVERSED: This card reversed suggests an end to love or that a love is not mutual. It can suggest volatility, frustration in love and marriage, lost love, falling out of love, lost attraction or a lack of sexual compatibility. It can warn that the other person has nothing to offer, that the inquirer should not expect love, tenderness or affection from them. It can signal a period of loneliness, or sadness. Only when associated with very strong positive cards could it indicate that a loveless period is ending.

OTHER CARD SYSTEMS: Four of Hearts

- Vera Sibilla: Four of Hearts: Love: feelings, blind force, expansion of tasks or activity

DATES: June 9 to 14

NUMBERS: 84 / 45

Lover

Original Italian title: *L'Amante*, the lover, masculine

This card is the male lover card. He is the ideal man, handsome, smart, and sincere.
- boyfriend, husband, lover
- devotion, adoration, loyalty
- acknowledgment of self-worth and inner value

SYMBOLS: This card shows a handsome well-dressed man playing a stringed instrument. He is wearing a red cape symbolizing the passion burning in his heart. He appears to be serenading someone with heartfelt songs of love. The setting is fairy-tale like; a tranquil courtyard, with flowers growing on the walls which could indicate that the environment around him is familiar and safe.

STRAIGHT: This card almost always gives a positive response to any question posed about love or a lover. The most common interpretation of this card is a person, a boyfriend, lover, husband, or sweetheart. This man is enchanted; he is in love and devoted. He is the boyfriend every mother wants for her daughter, the ideal husband for every bride. If the inquirer is male, this most likely represents him. However, it can also symbolize falling in love. It is an affirmation that love is near. The Lover promises improvements in love, life, work, health and happiness. When associated with negative cards, this card could suggest there is a rival. Associated with ending, or negative cards it could signify a breakup of a relationship.

SUGGESTIONS FOR:

LOVE: the perfect companion, honest, generous, sweet and sincere, long term partner to raise a family

WORK: a collaborator is capable, helpful, loyal and hardworking, multi-talented, flexible, sensitive and well prepared.

HEALTH: young doctor, nurse, masseuse or therapist can inspire hope and confidence.

ADVICE: Seize the moment, love is at hand. Your lover has come calling.

LOCATION IN CROSS SPREAD:

* Above – Past: a lover from your past is a contributing factor
* Below – Future: a potential love affair in the future, the right lover will be coming into your life
* In front – Obstacle: be grateful for this person who adores you
* Behind: Advice: be optimistic in matters of love, the answer is yes

REVERSED: This card is not overly negative when reversed. It is usually symbolic of immature love, uncertainty, confusion, doubts and questioning feelings. Only when associated with other negative cards could it indicate a bad person or it could indicate the removal of the beloved from the inquirer's life.

OTHER CARD SYSTEMS: Jack of Hearts
* Vera Sibilla: Jack of Hearts: Male Lover: young man, the inquirer or the inquirer's lover

DATES: January 29 to February 13

NUMBERS: None

Malady

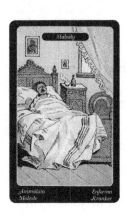

Original Italian title: *Ammalato*, sick

This is a negative card representing suffering or discomfort that could be either physical or emotional.

- illness, weakened state, disease
- inability to cope with a situation, burdened
- unpleasant changes

SYMBOLS: This card depicts a man, physically worn down and in bed. He is alone in the room, but there is a steaming cup and medicine on the nightstand. The solitude symbolizes the need to work through the disease alone. The medicine and remedy at hand is evidence that support and comfort is nearby and suggests that he will recover after a period of convalescence.

STRAIGHT: This card suggests that there is something "sick" resulting in suffering and requiring some time to pass before recovery can occur. The card refers to malady and not disease, thus it is about the state not the cause. The malady could be a physical ailment but more likely it refers to a situation. The "sickness" could be a flawed relationship due to bad behavior on the part of the inquirer or the other party. In love relationships, the malady could be due to a relationship being shallow, physical only, and not healthy. The situation could be communication that is flawed (rambling, misleading, confusing). The malady could also be loneliness, and the suffering of isolation or confinement.

SUGGESTIONS FOR:

LOVE: heartbreak, jealousy, envy, betrayal, injustice in love, suffering

WORK: slow progress, incomplete projects, confusion, turbulent relationships

HEALTH: sickness, disease, do not ignore symptoms, seek professional help

ADVICE: Take a break, a step back, and tend to the problem so healing can occur.

LOCATION IN CROSS SPREAD:

- Above – Past: there has been a period of suffering or confinement that has taken place
- Below – Future: a period of suffering is approaching
- In front – Obstacle: the challenge will be to endure, fight off the disease, find a remedy
- Behind: Advice: look for the cause for the malady in order to treat it.

REVERSED: This card is positive when reversed. This card takes on the meaning of "healing". It suggests the end of a period of confusion, sickness, hindrance. In the case of relationships, the two parties have come to their senses and resolved their issues which could be a misunderstanding, conflict, or other obstacle. If the inquiry is about physical ailments, this card suggests the end of a period of convalescence or the end of the reason for the malady.

OTHER CARD SYSTEMS: Four of Spades
- Vera Sibilla: Four of Spades : Sick Man: sickness, loneliness, solitude, unemployment

DATES: July 9 to 14

NUMBERS: 90 / 26

Melancholy

Original Italian title: *Malinconia,* melancholy

This card represents sadness, resignation and suffering with dignity.
- dwelling on mistakes, disappointments
- abandonment, depression, upset, grief
- anguish, anxiety, regrets

SYMBOLS: This card shows a solitary woman sitting on a bench. She looks thoughtful, her posture slouched over as if the weight of her thoughts is upon her. Behind her there is an almost bare tree, its leaves falling to the ground. The leaves signify hopes. Those fallen representing those that are lost, vulnerable to being swept away by winds and lost forever. Those still clinging to the branches, the last remaining hopes, are few and vulnerable. The woman is wearing a shawl which symbolizes her memories that she is wrapped up in.

STRAIGHT: This card refers to a state of being, one of sadness, heartache or loneliness. It suggests that the situation is one that is preoccupying the thoughts of the person at the center of the inquiry and as a result they are stuck, unable to move forward, or avoiding social interaction. It could be due to regrets, past mistakes, loss of a loved one, financial stresses or other great disappointment. This card is not overly negative because, whatever the situation, it implores the inquirer to gather their energies and move past it.

SUGGESTIONS FOR:
>LOVE: regret, resignation, sacrifice, trying to find strength to start again after separation
>WORK: need to pick up the pieces and start again
>HEALTH: difficult times but patient is well now, patience, will power and the patient will prevail

ADVICE: Accept the past, gather your thoughts, focus on what can be done to move beyond the situation.

LOCATION IN CROSS SPREAD:
- Above – Past: there has been a period of sadness and introspection
- Below – Future: you will need to process a mistake, regret or loss
- In front – Obstacle: the challenge will be to overcome the cause of melancholy
- Behind: Advice: gather yourself and move past the unhappy situation

REVERSED: This card reversed is only positive when associated with cards indicating an ending, suggesting the end of period of melancholy. This card reversed can be more negative as it suggests an emotional breakdown, a love gone wrong, an unhappy family situation, loss of a friendship, job or money. Association with love or wedding cards reinforces the negative interpretation as an irreversible break, an impossible situation, mourning for a loved one, a divorce or separation.

OTHER CARD SYSTEMS: Five of Diamonds
- Vera Sibilla: Five of Diamonds: Melancholy: loss of heart, temporary setback or sadness connected to the past

DATES: May 15 to 20

NUMBERS: 86 / 35

Merchant

Original Italian title: *Mercante*, merchant

This card represents success, ambition, business success and profits and can refer to a person or a situation.

- financial gain, profitable investments
- professional, successful businessman, skilled in business
- good business decisions, advantageous trade or negotiations
- cunning, crafty, greedy or devious

SYMBOLS: This card shows a merchant, with his wares, waiting on a pier. He appears to be gazing out to sea where, on the horizon, there is a ship. It suggests he is waiting to exchange his wares. He stands in a self-assured and confident pose, suggesting he is skilled in his business and that he knows the "ins and outs" and "tricks of the trade" to be successful. He is surrounded by goods, so he seems to be successful but one can't say if he is honest or dishonest as a merchant.

STRAIGHT: This card is considered a good omen in matters of business and trade and suggests an affirmative or positive answer to questions of success in business. This card is symbolic of skills in business, successful commerce, prosperous business and financial success. It can represent either a person or a situation. When it is a specific person, it indicates someone who successfully competes in business, selling, negotiation or investing. It can indicate someone who is a leader with foresight, good instincts and one who achieves success. Rarely is this card negative, however, when combined with negative cards is can suggest greed, cunning, stinginess, deceit or scheming.

SUGGESTIONS FOR:

LOVE: secret meetings, negotiation, financially beneficial marriages, marriage to an older man

WORK: favorable investments or negotiations, lucrative contracts, man in public eye, willing, sales success

HEALTH: tendency to gain weight, metabolic dysfunction

ADVICE: Have confidence, there will be success in business ventures or for key business associates.

LOCATION IN CROSS SPREAD:
- Above – Past: a successful business person or venture has had a significant impact
- Below – Future: relationship with a business person or business opportunity is possible
- In front – Obstacle: with success comes responsibility and pressure to continue
- Behind: Advice: Now is the time to negotiate, start a business or partner with a business person

REVERSED: When this card appears reversed, it suggests business failure. It is a warning against investing, starting a new venture, or negotiation. In matters of the heart, it suggests that negotiations will be in vain and things will not be favorable to the inquirer. Similarly, for friendships or work situations, one party is unable to hold up their end, or does not have the necessary skills or talents for success. If this card is associated with other negative cards, it can indicate defeat, financial difficulties, major setbacks or disappointment.

OTHER CARD SYSTEMS: Kind of Diamonds
- Vera Sibilla: King of Diamonds: Merchant: work, career, financial matters

DATES: January 11 to 20

NUMBERS: 79 / 12

65

Messenger

Original Italian title: *Messaggero*, messenger

This card represents the delivery of news or a message.

- announcement, results, invitation
- letter, phone call, email

SYMBOLS: The card shows a postman or courier delivering a letter to a woman. The personal delivery suggests that the news or message will be delivered not anonymously but by a person, and could be official in nature. This person could be a delivery person, friend, relative or acquaintance. The letter is symbolic, the message may come in any number of forms, not necessarily on paper. What is important is that the message reveals or announces important events or information that is useful or needed.

STRAIGHT: This card is usually considered positive. The Messenger card is an omen signaling the arrival of information. The information that has or will be delivered may arrive via phone, fax, email, mail, or courier and may come from a distant place or person. This card can also represent the arrival of the "messenger" and, in this context, the card could announce the arrival of a guest. When associated with "love" cards, it suggests paying attention to communication including the non-verbal signals between partners. In matters of work or career, this card usually signals good news unless it is associated with negative cards.

SUGGESTIONS FOR:

LOVE: news of love either positive or negative, letter or phone call from friends or relatives, visit by a dear person

WORK: time for action, send quotes and proposals, changes coming, new offers, meetings to attend

HEALTH: results are available, assessment, diagnosis or opinion from physician is available

ADVICE: Pay attention and consider the content of the message before making your next move.

LOCATION IN CROSS SPREAD:

- Above – Past: consider carefully the information you have already received
- Below – Future: the information you are waiting for is coming.
- In front – Obstacle: information is needed or needs to be provided in order to move forward
- Behind: Advice: look for the message and consider the information before making a choice

REVERSED: This card reversed suggests that the message or information that the inquirer wants or needs is not coming. This reversal is generally considered a negative or "no" answer. However, it may not be due to the action of the inquirer, but rather the inaction of the one who should be delivering the message. In this case, it may reveal attributes of the messenger, that they are lazy, ineffective in their work or superficial. If the inquirer is waiting for a love interest to express their feelings or a profession of love, it will not come in the near term if at all. It is possible that this card reversed is positive if the inquirer is waiting for bad news. In this case, it indicates that the bad news is not coming.

OTHER CARD SYSTEMS: Jack of Diamonds
- Vera Sibilla: Jack of Diamonds: Messenger: communication, usually official communication, a postman, mediator

DATES: January 21 to 31

NUMBERS: 71 / 19

Misfortune

Original Italian title: *Disgrazia*, disgrace

This is a negative card symbolizing calamity, ruin, or catastrophe.
- disgrace, fall from grace
- accident, mishap
- sudden, unexpected, unpredicted negative event

SYMBOLS: This card shows a man falling from a burning building. A firefighter tires to extinguish the fire but the building is engulfed in flames and collapsing. No one can enter the building and thus there is no help for anyone within, no rescue, no escape. The collapsing building is symbolic of complete destruction in the wake of the catastrophic event.

STRAIGHT: This is a negative card suggesting an accident, failure or serious problem. It can suggest loss of love, loss of a job, the failure of a business venture, or an error that results in grave consequences. This card almost always suggests that there will be a change for the worse, a lost cause, an unrecoverable or irreparable loss. This could include foreclosure, debt or deep rift in a relationship. It also warns that there is little that anyone can do to prevent or mitigate the situation, the inquirer will be left to deal with the situation on their own. This card amplifies associated negative cards. When associated with very positive cards it might signal that complete destruction is needed in order to start again with a new foundation. Out of the ashes, something new and wonderful will emerge.

SUGGESTIONS FOR:

LOVE: legal separation or divorce, loss of family property, lawsuits regarding inheritance or disputes between relatives
WORK: time of great difficulty, dismissal, bankruptcy, difficult time professionally, no help from colleagues
HEALTH: accident, illness, mental disorders, depression, loss of contact with reality

ADVICE: Recognize that things are ending and forever changed. You will need to rebuild.

LOCATION IN CROSS SPREAD:
- Above – Past: have been dealing with a devastating loss or accident.
- Below – Future: a time of great difficulty is ahead
- In front – Obstacle: there will be significant difficulties to overcome
- Behind: Advice: do not give up in the face of significant difficulties, be prepared to rebuild

REVERSED: When reversed, this card is significantly more negative in that it suggests that the irreparable loss is an ending with a finality that will significantly impact the inquirer. It suggests a painful event that destroys hopes for the future. Only if this card is associated with past negative and positive future cards, such as wedding, love, or consolation, does it suggest an end of the misfortune and a resurgence of hope.

OTHER CARD SYSTEMS: Seven of Spades
- Vera Sibilla: Seven of Spades: Disgrace: ending, argument, wrath, accident, surgery, break, damage
- Tarot: The Tower: destruction, necessity, cleansing, foundation

DATES: October 28 to November 1

NUMBERS: 56 / 17

69

Money

Original Italian title: *Denaro*, money

This is a positive card symbolizing money, abundance, and good fortune.
- inheritance, winnings, luck
- success and prosperity are within reach
- confidence, self-worth, success

SYMBOLS: This card depicts a room filled with money. There is money on the table and also in a large open safe in the wall. The large quantity of money visible symbolizes abundance. The open safe could symbolize the need for saving or having to access savings. There is an empty chair by the table which serves as a reminder that money does not bring happiness or love. There are other items with the money that could be wills or other documents of great value or concerning money. All these valuables clearly visible, could symbolize assessing or taking stock of all that is available because there is a pressing need or shortfall to cover. The safe can also be a symbol of the heart, where hopes for the future and secrets are stored.

STRAIGHT: The appearance of this card is considered positive, an omen of financial good fortune and well-being. The source of the wealth can come from family, winnings or business sources. It also reminds the inquirer that it is important to save because fortunes can change and savings can become depleted. If this card is associated with "fortune" it symbolizes great wealth. If this card is associated with a card symbolizing a desire, such as home, it suggests that the funds needed to acquire it will be found. If associated with cards concerning love, it can warn of the material nature of a relationship or that the love interest is motivated by money. If this card is associated with cards suggesting interruption in the future, it signals a time of financial challenges approaching and that money will be lost or scarce.

SUGGESTIONS FOR:
LOVE: unions, marriages, partnerships or affairs have financial motivations, be wary of gold diggers
WORK: difficult financial challenges, need for more capital, investment or payment delays
HEALTH: there may be a need to tap savings to pay for medical expenses in order to get better

ADVICE: Material wealth can be fleeting, make sure to save for future needs.

LOCATION IN CROSS SPREAD:
- Above – Past: the situation has been financially secure, a time of abundance
- Below – Future: a time of abundance and financial security is coming
- In front – Obstacle: the need or desire for money is a factor in this situation
- Behind: advice: avoid being wasteful or not saving for the future when times are good

REVERSED: This card reversed signals a loss of money, which could be due to gambling, money wasted or spent in vain. It is only interpreted as positive when revered if it is associated with an "ending" card signaling the end of period of stagnation, poverty, misery, or financial hardship. In most cases, though, it is a warning that there will be complications as a result of inadequate funding. This can be due to the inquirer spending too much, squandering an inheritance, depleting savings or making poor investment choices. It advises that the time of plenty is over and that it is time to be frugal and conserve resources. If the inquirer is waiting for a sum of money, it is likely that it will not come

OTHER CARD SYSTEMS:
- Vera Sibilla: Six of Hearts: Money: assets, financial gain, the past.

DATES: September 21 to 27

NUMBERS: 49 / 30

Old Woman

Original Italian title: *Vecchia Signora*, old lady

This is a positive card representing a wise and trustworthy person or serene family environment.
- mother, grandmother, aunt, female professor, mature woman
- positive, reassuring, good advice
- intuition, wisdom

SYMBOLS: This card shows a woman with gray hair sitting in an armchair. She has a blanket across her lap and a book in her hand. The book, either for reading or praying suggests knowledge and devotion. The surrounding room appears to be a home that is serene and well cared for. There is a lamp and a vase of flowers on the table beside her. The lamp symbolizes shining a light to illuminate the matter or light the way. The vase with the simple single flower symbolizes a mature love, modest but beautiful.

STRAIGHT: This card can represent either a person or an atmosphere. It can represent a wise woman, who provides good advice and counsel. This card suggests that the inquirer should look to and trust the advice of an older woman. This card can also represent good advice derived from experience, wisdom or intuition that comes from someone of any age. It can also represent the inner voice or intuition of the inquirer. If associated with marriage cards, it can refer to a mother-in-law or other matriarch. When it refers to a situation, it can represent a peaceful, traditional family environment. This card is usually positive and can indicate family harmony or traditional values.

SUGGESTIONS FOR:
LOVE: valuable advice will come from a mature woman to help manage a relationship with a loved one
WORK: a mature colleague will be of special assistance, advice from an older woman will be valuable
HEALTH: the health of an older family member may be failing or an older family member will care for the inquirer

ADVICE: Listen for the voice of wisdom.

LOCATION IN CROSS SPREAD:
- Above – Past: there has been important advice from a wise woman
- Below – Future: there will be advice, council or the wisdom of experience to call upon
- In front – Obstacle: traditional values and conventional wisdom may be a challenge
- Behind: Advice: seek out and listen to advice and wisdom

REVERSED: Reversed this card suggests that the old woman will not be supportive, will provide bad, advice, meddle, interfere or otherwise disrupt the situation. This card can also suggest that a situation is stuck in the past, outdated, or deteriorating. It may also warn the inquirer of narrow mindedness, out of date ideas, or an unwillingness to seek advice or change. It is not generally considered an overly negative card when reversed unless it is associated with other negative cards such as "Malady", "Melancholy" or "Death". With significant negative cards, it could indicate a serious loss of health or death of an older woman.

OTHER CARD SYSTEMS: Two of Spades
- Vera Sibilla: Two of Spades: Old Lady: older woman, ex, old fashioned people or opinions, attachment to past

DATES: June 28 to July 2

NUMBERS: None

Pleasure Seekers

Original Italian title: *I Deliranti*, the delirious

This card can represent either people or an attribute. It can represent a group partying or disorderly, drunken or delusional behavior.

- exuberance, spirited
- situation is out of control
- group of friends

SYMBOLS: This card shows three young men in civilian clothes. They appear to be drunk, supporting each other and perhaps shouting or singing. The group looks like they are having fun in a delirious, crazy or wild manner.

STRAIGHT: The interpretation of this card is very dependent on adjacent cards and the nature of the inquiry. When associated with positive cards like Cheerfulness or Fortune it can indicate a party or a fun but disorderly gathering of friends. When associated with negative cards it can represent crazy thoughts, agitation, recklessness, or delirium. Getting carried away, being swept up in the crowd or being negatively influenced by peers are also possible interpretations. This card warns that there could be confusion, misunderstandings, delusions, or crazy behavior.

SUGGESTIONS FOR:
    LOVE: risky relationships or behavior, lack of respect, delusions about the situation
    WORK: colleagues are not serious or supportive, situation is degrading
    HEALTH: it is a particularly difficult time that is obvious to others, mental defects or delusions

ADVICE: Be aware that, with exuberance, reckless choices or errors in judgment are possible.

LOCATION IN CROSS SPREAD:
- Above – Past: previous reckless behavior may have had consequences
- Below – Future: a gathering or period of risky behavior is possible
- In front – Obstacle: the challenge will be to avoid delusions, resist being drawn into risky behavior
- Behind: Advice: do not be reckless or errors in judgment could result

REVERSED: This card reversed suggests a behavior that leads nowhere or significant errors in judgment. It also suggests a state of confusion. It warns that there will be difficulties and defeat due to unwise behavior, useless action, counterproductive discussions, or incompetence. The advice of this card revered is to assess actions and behaviors to determine the underlying cause and to adjust in order to avoid a negative outcome.

OTHER CARD SYSTEMS: Nine of Diamonds
- Vera Sibilla: Nine of Diamonds: Madmen: setbacks, irregularity, inconsistency, false point of view, bad influence

DATES: September 8 to 14

NUMBERS: 85 / 43

Priest

Original Italian title: *Sacerdote*, priest

This is a thematic card symbolizing values, sacredness, and justice.

- spirituality, morality, beliefs
- ecclesiastic person, confessor
- legal opinions, regulations, decisions

SYMBOLS: The central figure of this card is a young priest. The priest represents someone sacred, representing God and the laws of the church or society. He is someone who preaches about what is good or evil, right or wrong, just or unjust. The figure is well dressed suggesting that he is privileged which could symbolize the duality of what is being preached versus the actions of the person preaching. The priest appears to be reading from his breviary, suggesting that what he preaches is not coming from him. The church in the background emphasizes the sacred while the clock tower is a reminder of the passing of time who's only master is God or fate.

STRAIGHT: This is a neutral card that symbolizes the presence of the sacred, that there is a higher power and there are universal laws defining what is good versus what is evil. This card can be a suggestion to examine one's conscience and reminds of personal responsibility for thoughts and actions. This card is a reminder that there is more to life than the physical of this world. As a thematic card, it can suggest that there are pressing legal matters that require attention. Rarely does this card refer to a specific person, however, if other cards lead to this interpretation, the youth and inexperience of the one preaching may be the message that this card is conveying.

SUGGESTIONS FOR:
LOVE: a legal opinion will be needed to proceed with separation or inheritance
WORK: difficulties are coming possibly due to "sins" of the inquirer, judgment, legal issues are looming
HEALTH: poor medical reports, possible serious illness necessitating calling the priest

ADVICE: Make an honest assessment of recent actions and thoughts. Choose the right, moral or just option.

LOCATION IN CROSS SPREAD:
* Above – Past: you will be judged based on past actions
* Below – Future: judgment or spiritual guidance will be needed
* In front – Obstacle: the challenge will be to choose the just or right path
* Behind: Advice: act responsibly lest you be judged harshly

REVERSED: When this card is reversed, the interpretation is more straightforward. It suggests loss of morality, injustice, prejudice, and errors in judgment. It can also suggest the presence of an immoral or treacherous individual. When associated with cards showing hazards, it can suggest the occult. For economic situations, this card reversed signifies miscalculations, squandering of resources, or investment errors. For work situations, it can signal a dissatisfied boss, poor judgment or being judged. It is a warning against a wild and immoral life, spiritual confusion, vengeance, lack of forgiveness or other "evils'.

OTHER CARD SYSTEMS: King of Spades
* Vera Sibilla: Priest: authority, law, emotional coldness, emotional unavailability

DATES: March 14 to 20

NUMBERS: 74 / 40

Prison

Original Italian title: *Prigione*, prison

This card is a negative theme card symbolizing mental or physical confinement.
- difficulty moving on
- shame, guilt, self-punishment
- a period of anxiety, regret, remorse
- exile, loneliness

SYMBOLS: A prison is a place of punishment, despair, loneliness and confinement. This card shows a man in chains in a prison, alone and cut off from the world, behind bars. He is well dressed, holding his head in his hands, perhaps feeling remorse or regret. In the lower right corner there is a pitcher, symbolizing what is needed to survive the confinement, loneliness and solitude.

STRAIGHT: This card most commonly symbolizes something locked, closed or the inability to break free. This could be related to actual punishment or justice but more likely it is related to spiritual or emotional conditions. This card can symbolize taking time to think and meditate on mistakes. This confinement could be self-imposed so it could indicate there is an inability to move forward, either through stubbornness or being imprisoned by a person or a situation. This card suggests that the condition or circumstances are not permanent, it is a temporary state that once the sentence is over, the person will be free.

78

SUGGESTIONS FOR:
LOVE: closure, tears and sadness, solitude suggesting end of a relationship or grave misunderstandings
WORK: difficult times, creative blocks, economic constraints
HEALTH: unfavorable clinical results, concern is warranted

ADVICE: Take responsibility and acknowledge your wrongdoings; this will set you free.

LOCATION IN CROSS SPREAD:
- Above – Past: there has been a time of loneliness, punishment or confinement
- Below – Future: there will be a difficult period of feeling trapped or restrained
- In front – Obstacle: the challenge will be to move past the situation when the time comes
- Behind: Advice: take responsibility for your actions

REVERSED: When reversed, this card suggests that the term of punishment has ended. It can still be a negative situation, but the inquirer has been released from some confining circumstance or situation. Closed mindedness, prejudice, negative thoughts, regrets and remorse are all possible restraints that could be lifted when this card appears reversed. It's most positive interpretation is being freed from a negative situation.

OTHER CARD SYSTEMS: Nine of Spades
- Vera Sibilla: Nine of Spades: Prison: blockage, obligation, pregnancy

DATES: November 8 to 14

NUMBERS: 70 / 14

Reunion

Original Italian title: *La Riunione*, the reunion

This card represents a meeting; a positive encounter that results in a new beginning.
- appointment, invitation to meet, business meeting
- clarification, resolution
- a fresh start, satisfactory solution for all parties

SYMBOLS: This card shows an elegantly attired man and woman. The woman appears to be a bit shy, but the scene is tender and couple's closeness implies a relationship of some intimacy. The man appears to be a gentleman as he holds her extended hand in a respectful manner. His attentiveness and demeanor suggest he is courting the woman. The backdrop is a forest which is a symbol of a reserved or private place and it is significant that this meeting takes place in such a setting. The surrounding forest is very green symbolizing hope.

STRAIGHT: This card indicates an encounter or meeting will take place that results in clarification, resolution or a fresh start. This meeting could be between lovers, separated either by a break in communication or an actual breakup. This card is a very positive omen for reconciliation between lovers separated for whatever reason and confirms the return of the beloved. It can represent a meeting between friends or family members that "clears the air" and where conflicts or differences are resolved. It could also represent a business meeting to resolve a conflict, begin a new project or resume a partnership. It can indicate that an invitation to such a meeting is possible or that there is something important that will need to be discussed in order to move forward. This is almost always a positive card, especially if associated with love, hope or money cards or with cards indicating progress or movement.

SUGGESTIONS FOR:
LOVE: resolution is needed, misunderstandings give way to new understanding, love and passion returns
WORK: interview for a new job, meetings with company leaders that results in success
HEALTH: seek professional counseling to resolve inner conflict, consultation between health care professionals

ADVICE: Reconnect with others to achieve reconciliation and success.

LOCATION IN CROSS SPREAD:
- Above – Past: a recent reunion or meeting has brought people together
- Below – Future: a meeting with the potential for resolution or reconciliation will occur
- In front – Obstacle: there are misunderstandings that need to be discussed in order to move forward
- Behind: Advice: look for an opportunity to reconnect with others and success will come, make a fresh start

REVERSED: When reversed, this card suggests a missed or postponed appointment or meeting or one that the inquirer has been avoiding. For business situations, reversed, this card suggests a failure to resolve a situation or an important meeting that will not take place. It can also warn that there will be no explanation or that reconciliation will not happen. It can suggest that there is an impediment to travel, especially if associated with "Journey" or other movement cards. When associated with cards suggesting danger or hazard, it could mean a meeting will go poorly.

OTHER CARD SYSTEMS: Eight of Clubs
- Vera Sibilla: Eight of Clubs: Gathering: meeting, date, reconciliation, getting back together, progress, healing, improvement, two or more of something

DATES: August 2 to 7

NUMBERS: 60 / 4

Room

Original Italian title: *Stanza*, room

This neutral card represents a private tranquil place or state of being, where one can gather their thoughts or meet with someone in an intimate setting.

- intimacy, privacy
- receiving guests, being welcomed by others
- need to retreat or reflect
- waiting for something to happen, someone to arrive

SYMBOLS: The card pictures a nicely decorated room. The room looks like it is in a home suggesting that it is a private space. The color suggests it is a warm and tranquil space. There is no one in the room but the empty chair symbolizes anticipation or waiting for someone to arrive to occupy it. The windows of the room are closed, blocking out whatever is outside, perhaps isolating those who occupy the room and keeping them from understanding or seeing what's going on around them.

STRAIGHT: This card describes an atmosphere that is tranquil and orderly. Everything is in its place but there is a feeling that something or someone is missing from the picture. It can suggest there is a need to retreat and reflect in order to make sense of a situation. This card can also suggest a need for confidential talks, intimate encounters or private meetings. The associated cards can bring understanding to what needs clarification or what the inquirer should be thinking about doing. With regards to love relationships, it can suggest a need for intimacy, boredom or a need to re-evaluate the relationship. It can also mean that there is a person that should be present, that is, the inquirer is waiting for someone to arrive. "Room" combined with other cards can indicate the type of room, as examples, with: "Journey" a hotel room, "Child" a nursery, "Malady" a hospital room, "Doctor" a consultation room.

SUGGESTIONS FOR:
LOVE: intimacy between lovers, love or sex in privacy, serene moments or meetings between family members or friends
WORK: positive outcomes, proven ability, business conducted in orderly manner
HEALTH: health is not a problem, high energy and sexual desire

ADVICE: Take advantage of the serenity of this moment either alone or with someone special.

LOCATION IN CROSS SPREAD:
- Above – Past: things have been tranquil and serene, there has been time for introspection or intimate encounters
- Below – Future: there will be privacy for either confidential meetings or personal refection
- In front – Obstacle: the challenge will be to reflect on what or who is missing from your surroundings
- Behind: Advice: make the most of the privacy and tranquility of this time and space

REVERSED: This card reversed signifies a world turned upside down. This can be inner turmoil, confusion or loss of perspective. It can indicate impulsive behavior, not getting ahead of a situation before it gets messy or the inability to get things back on track. It suggests that the situation is complex and tangled, full of obstacles and relationships that are complicated and distorted. It can also refer to a material loss of a home, office or property. When associated with "Wedding" or other love cards, it could indicate betrayal, deception, lack of love, or disorder in the relationship. If the inquiry pertains to work or business, this card reversed suggests a negative response or outcome, false hope, or contrary conditions.

OTHER CARD SYSTEMS: Ace of Diamonds
- Vera Sibilla: Ace of Diamonds: Intimacy, private sphere, private communication, communication of secrets, economic success and improvement.

DATES: April 21 to 27
NUMBERS: None

Scholar

Original Italian title: *Letterato*, man of letters

This card symbolizes an older, knowledgeable person.
- expert, connoisseur, wise councilor, professor
- guidance, wisdom, experience, intellect

SYMBOLS: The central figure of this card is an older man, sitting in an armchair reading a large book. The surroundings include a table and a large bookcase, suggesting the room is a library or study. His age and the setting combined suggest he has wisdom and experience. He appears to be intently reading, concentrating on the subject matter, studying, or analyzing suggesting he is a scholar or highly educated person who is not easily distracted.

STRAIGHT: This card usually represents a person, a well-educated, trusted advisor. This is a person of culture, knowledge and status. This is also a person that can be trusted, not only for their knowledge and wise council but also their discretion. This person knows the facts, is well informed or is the friend who can get to the heart of the matter. This person is generally calm, sensitive, serious and understands the value of silence rather than talking too much. They are one who uses their strength of reason rather than physical strength.

SUGGESTIONS FOR:
LOVE: there may be a crisis in a relationship, a wise person will provide council to restore harmony
WORK: a solution will be found through wisdom and knowledge, help could come from a scholar or from within
HEALTH: worry will end, problems will be identified and solved with accurate diagnosis

ADVICE: Use logic and reason to solve the problem at hand.

LOCATION IN CROSS SPREAD:
- Above – Past: a person with wisdom and experience has provided valuable guidance
- Below – Future: there will be someone with relevant knowledge and experience who can provide guidance
- In front – Obstacle: resolution will require the inquirer to seek wisdom and knowledge from a trusted advisor
- Behind: Advice: seek guidance from a trusted source or make decisions using knowledge and wisdom

REVERSED: When reversed this card indicates a lack of preparation, lack of study, or the failure of an examination or application. It can also represent lack of consideration in ordinary activities, nonsense, or illogical, uncivilized, rude, or arrogant behavior. In work or career situations, this card reversed indicates a lack of training or preparation in order to achieve success. If this card reversed is associated with negative cards, the lack of knowledge, skills or wisdom is likely the cause of the negative outcome.

OTHER CARD SYSTEMS: Seven of Hearts
- Vera Sibilla: Seven of Hearts: Artist: intellectual, educated person, artist, attorney, contract, good news

DATES: September 28 to October 2

NUMBERS: 67 / 10

Servant

Original Italian title: *Donna di Servizio*, woman of service

This is a positive card representing a female person, generous by nature, who provides support and service.

- professional, faithful, respectful
- household staff, secretaries, support staff
- caring, sweet, sensible, modest

SYMBOLS: This card shows a woman, dressed as a maid, serving drinks on a tray. The maid symbolizes a caregiver, a person of trust who takes care of daily routines and needs. The setting is domestic, symbolizing that the service is provided in a friendly, comfortable environment.

STRAIGHT: This card is positive in that it suggests the presence of someone who is loyal, respectful and will provide help and service or collaboration. It also suggests that the service is provided in a friendly, hospitable way that makes the recipient very comfortable. The card indicates that there is someone close by who is or will continue to take care of the inquirer. This card also warns that this service is provided for compensation, and that the inquirer should be cautious to surround themselves with people who are true and sincere.

SUGGESTIONS FOR:
LOVE: the presence of an honest reliable comforting woman, mother, lover, sister, wife, friend
WORK: reliable person who does their job well, collaborator, colleague, help to achieve success
HEALTH: nurse, social worker, devoted to others without personal interest

ADVICE: Accept help from a trusted person to resolve the situation or achieve your goals.

LOCATION IN CROSS SPREAD:
- Above – Past: someone has provided support and help to get to this point
- Below – Future: help will be available, likely from a female person
- In front – Obstacle: the challenge will be to seek out the right help and support
- Behind: Advice: accept help in order to achieve your goals

REVERSED: Reversed this card suggests that there is a betrayal of trust or an employee that takes advantage, unproductive or lazy. Instead of providing support and help, this person works against the inquirer. It can also signal that the inquirer is unable or unwilling to accept help or a lack of self-care. This card reversed almost always signals an uncomfortable situation or difficult times because help is not available.

OTHER CARD SYSTEMS: Eight of Diamonds
- Vera Sibilla: Three of Diamonds: Handmaid: employed woman, gift, everything that is given or granted.

DATES: May 3 to 8

NUMBERS: 53 / 21

Service

Original Italian title: *Domestico*, servant

This card represents a male person who provides help and service.

- receiving help or offering help to others
- well-mannered, respectful, dutiful, helpful staff
- work

SYMBOLS: The card shows a man who appears to be a footman, doorman or hotel porter. He is opening the door of a carriage, presumably to assist the occupant within. His posture seems reverent, servile, and typical for a man of service but he does not seem very happy. The man represents those who support us and make everyday life easier.

STRAIGHT: This card is positive in that it suggests that help is available to the inquirer. However, this card can be interpreted in a number of ways. The first is that help comes from someone who provides service because they are a loyal friend, devoted and caring. This person can be trusted as they come to the aid of the inquirer willingly. Conversely, the person could be helping because it is their job to do so, they do so out of self-interest, for personal gain rather than out of love or loyalty. In some cases this card can represent the work of the inquirer, the services they provide whether paid or not. The associated cards will need to be consulted to determine which of the two interpretations is most likely. When this card is associated with love cards, the inquirer should question whether or not the person is there to help out of love or because they have something to gain from the situation. The same is true for questions regarding work or business. Evaluation of the associated cards will be needed to determine if business associates are there out of devotion and loyalty to the enterprise or for personal gain. If surrounding cards are positive, then the inquirer will receive help and service from a devoted husband, boyfriend, good and loyal servants, a business partner of good moral character, or a faithful friend.

SUGGESTIONS FOR:

LOVE: your feelings are not wrong, motives are unclear, a partner may not be supportive

WORK: do not trust blindly those who work for you, listen more, be clear with contracts and documentation

HEALTH: get a second opinion on health matters, there may be reason to doubt the service you receive

ADVICE: Accept help with gratitude while being mindful of the motivations of the one serving.

LOCATION IN CROSS SPREAD:
- Above – Past: help, support or work is a contributing factor
- Below – Future: there will be help available, you will need to evaluate motivations
- In front – Obstacle: the challenge will be to accept help with gratitude or to assess a work situation
- Behind: Advice: be mindful of the motivations of those who serve

REVERSED: This card reversed is negative in that it suggests that not only will help not arrive, but that there may be an enemy disguised as a friend. It warns of someone who undermines the inquirer's efforts, a rival in the workplace, or a loved one that is working at crossed purposes. It can also suggest the presence of someone who appears to be helpful but is, in reality, harmful. It warns of the presence of someone two-faced, an unfaithful friend, a dishonest employee, or someone who is disloyal. Associated with love cards, it could indicate the love is false, with no real roots or motivated by greed or convenience. Reversed, this card can also point to the inquirer's motivations, raising the question of whether or not their heart is in their work.

OTHER CARD SYSTEMS: Jack of Clubs
- Vera Sibilla: Jack of Clubs: Servant: young man, co-worker, employee, dutiful, helpful

DATES: November 21 to December 3

NUMBERS: None

Sighs

Original Italian title: *Sospiri*, sighing

This card represents the emotions, thoughts, worries or anxieties experienced while waiting for an answer or after a negative answer.

- searching for an answer or solution
- anticipation, expectation
- isolation, abandonment, loneliness
- separated, divorced, widowed

SYMBOLS: The central figure of this card is a woman sitting by the sea. She is visibly sad and appears to be waiting or thinking serious thoughts. She is dressed in black which represents mourning or sadness. She is holding a card in her hand, perhaps a message from someone special or maybe a ticket for a voyage not taken. On the ground, there is a red rose, symbolizing love, suggesting that matters of the heart are the reason for her sighs. There is a ship in the background which symbolizes arrivals, departures, or news.

STRAIGHT: This card is considered positive as it represents sentimental thoughts of someone or something. However, these thoughts and feelings can be positive or negative; the anticipation of an arrival or the sadness of a departure. In matters of the heart, this card can represent "sighs of love", those emotions that swirl when there is uncertainty or waiting for a loved one. This card speaks to the emotional response we have when someone or something has value or is "worth it". In work or business situations, this card suggests there is an expectation of news or results that will impact the outcome. This card can also represent the thoughts and anxiety of not knowing the answer, when the solution or outcome is unknown. Even when the situation is negative, it is not devastating anxiety, rather, it is thoughts or regrets about how things could have been done for a different outcome. It can also suggest there is a woman who loves and admires the inquirer. This woman could be a wife, lover or secret admirer.

SUGGESTIONS FOR:
LOVE: desire for passion and love, worries or anxiety about a relationship
WORK: doubts about what to do, job is unfulfilling, hard to find a way out of the situation
HEALTH: impatient for recovery, must not give up hope rather trust in the care being given

ADVICE: The time will come when you must leave your cares behind and move on.

LOCATION IN CROSS SPREAD:
- Above – Past: there have been thoughts and feelings about someone or something wished for
- Below – Future: a time of longing and introspection is ahead
- In front – Obstacle: the challenge will be to know when to move on from this situation
- Behind: Advice: don't let your thoughts keep you from action

REVERSED: Reversed this card indicates the end of a time of waiting for something desired. The "sighs" for something or someone are over. The associated cards are necessary to give clarification. The anxiety may have passed because the desired person has returned, a wish has been granted or dream come true. Conversely, it could mean that there is no hope, that feelings of love are unrequited, or a dream has vanished. It can also suggest there is discouragement or denial about a situation or refusal to take responsibility for a situation. If the inquirers question is in regard to a female lover, it is possible she no longer "sighs" for them.

OTHER CARD SYSTEMS: Six of Spades
- Vera Sibilla: Six of Spades: Sighs: waiting, expectation, anxiety

DATES: October 21 to 27

NUMBERS: 63 / 38

Soldier

Original Italian title: *Militare*, military

This card represents someone in authority or the attributes of strength, protectiveness, suspicion, or precision.

- military, officer, young professional
- on guard against hostility, protection
- justice, honor, investigation

SYMBOLS: The central figure on this card is an armed uniformed soldier. He is standing guard in front of a fort with a flag blowing in the wind. The man is young and vital symbolizing masculinity, but also youthful fervor, purity of intention, commitment and dedication. The solider has a defensive and protective posture, indicating he is prepared to do battle if necessary.

STRAIGHT: The interpretation of this card is influenced by the situation and the associated cards. The most general meaning is that of a person, a soldier, a policeman, or someone in a position of authority. When it is not an individual, it represents the attributes of suspicion, jealousy, mistrust, protectiveness, or defensiveness. It can also signify justice or enforcement of laws. In business situations, this card can be interpreted as a faithful partner, or trustworthy employees. When associated with other positive cards, this card can take on a more positive meaning, one of protection, serious commitment, and practical support. In love, it can be someone who does not have a lot of confidence, is picky, or someone that does not trust easily. If followed by reversed love cards, it suggests that the relationship was not right for one of the parties but "fate" has put things on the correct path.

SUGGESTIONS FOR:
LOVE: relationship will need to be defended from outside influences, your lover is serious and protective
WORK: work concerns, colleagues on the defensive, conflict is possible
HEALTH: need to be proactive about health, if suspect something should seek professional advice

ADVICE: When faced with opposition, seek to resolve conflicts before they escalate. Look to those who stand up for you for help.

LOCATION IN CROSS SPREAD:
- Above - Past: consider the impact discipline, protection or authority has had
- Below – Future: a person of authority, a protective person, or an attitude of justice or defense will influence the situation
- In front – Obstacle: be aware of outside forces, evaluate if they are protective or defensive
- Behind - Advice: allow someone trusted to protect you, resolve conflicts before they escalate

REVERSED: There are also two distinct interpretations of this card when it appears reversed. The first is a lack of protection, lack of help, friends who are not trustworthy or cannot be counted on. The second is an untrustworthy person, someone who does not provide protection or is jealous, possessive, controlling, confining or restricting. It can also suggest an unjust situation or person that keeps one from moving forward or hinders the development of a relationship. In business, reversed, this card suggests fierce competition or disloyal employees. If associated with the "Thief", it warns the inquirer that there is someone who will seriously harm the inquirer.

OTHER CARD SYSTEMS: Ten of Spades
- Vera Sibilla: Ten of Spades: Soldier, violence, force, people in uniform, aggressive, inhospitable places, secrets

DATES: November 15 to 20
NUMBERS: 61 / 7

Sorrow

Original Italian title: *Dispiacere*, displeasure

This card symbolizes sorrow and loss.
- profound sadness, anguish, pain, grief
- separation, broken heart
- serious problems of money or health

SYMBOLS: This card shows a woman who is clearly in anguish. She is draped over a column at the base of a stairway leading up to a villa. There is a blue scarf draped over her and hiding the head of the figure carved into the column. The color blue symbolizes sadness and the draping symbolizes inconsolability. There is a note or letter at her elbow, suggesting that bad news has come that has thrown this woman into turmoil and despair. There is a large rose bush nearby and a single flower is separated and on the ground nearby which could be a statement that something once alive and vibrant is now permanently separated and dying. In the background is the sea, it is calm and the sky is not ominous symbolizing that the news has come suddenly "out of the blue".

STRAIGHT: This is a negative card suggesting serious obstacles or sudden misfortune that bring sadness. What is important to consider with the appearance of this card is the cause of the distress. It may be due to the arrival of bad news but if could be distress due to a wide variety of causes. The associated cards may give clues to the source and severity of the sorrow. If associated with love cards, such as "Wedding", it could suggest widowhood, divorce or separation. If the associated cards are not particularly negative, the sorrow may be less severe or it is the displeasure or sorrow of someone else that is affecting the inquirer. If the associated cards are negative in nature, the problem maybe more serious, irreversible, even fatal, resulting in inconsolable grief.

SUGGESTIONS FOR:
    LOVE: grief at loss of a loved one, broken marriage, relationship or engagement, family argument
    WORK: loss of job, bad relationships with colleagues or boss, economic concerns
    HEALTH: serious health concerns for self or a loved one, exhaustion, depression

ADVICE: Even in times of profound sadness, look for a positive direction to channel your thoughts and energy.

LOCATION IN CROSS SPREAD:
- Above – Past: a loss or period of sorrow has occurred recently
- Below – Future: an event could suddenly occur that causes grief for the inquirer
- In front – Obstacle: the challenge will be to move beyond a significant loss or misfortune that has caused great sorrow
- Behind: Advice: do not give in to despair

REVERSED: This card reversed in the past or present part of a spread signals that pain, disappointment or sorrow has or will soon come to an end. Due to its emotional nature, this card reversed can also suggest madness or a sense that the "sky is falling". When "Sorrow" reversed is associated with significant negative cards, it can magnify the sorrow and suggest misfortune, death, or serious economic stress. With negative cards, the seriousness of the sorrow makes it one of the most negative cards in the deck and warns the inquirer of significant challenges on the horizon.

OTHER CARD SYSTEMS: Ace of Spades
- Vera Sibilla: Ace of Spades: Sorrow: bad news, sorrow, violence, failure

DATES: June 21 to 27

NUMBERS: 64 / 9

Surprise

Original Italian title: *Consolante Sorpresa,*
consoling surprise

This card represents a surprise, unexpected joy
or positive event.

- unexpected money, reward, win, bonus
- surprise visit, letter, or phone call
- good news or lucky break, success

SYMBOLS: The card shows a man who appears to have thrown
a small net into a river. Although the man has made the initial
effort, by throwing his net into the river, he seems to have caught
something unexpected and surprisingly good. The man is not
struggling to collect this surprise catch, it comes easily to him and
he appears happy and at ease. The pastoral countryside setting also
suggests peace and tranquility surrounds him. The green color that
is predominant in the card symbolizes hope and rebirth.

STRAIGHT: This is a positive card that suggests a happy surprise.
The positive outcome is a product of something the inquirer has
done, although the result is unexpected or better than expected.
This card also suggests the realization of a desire, the unexpected
fulfillment of something that was hoped for but was not expected
to happen. It is always, as the card is captioned, a surprise. The
surprise could come in the form of a small win, an exam passed, a
new job, written correspondence, a personal encounter, a bonus,
money or something recovered that was considered lost. This
is a card that brings some unexpected relief to any situation.
The associated cards provide an indication of the circumstances
surrounding the surprise. This card also suggests a peaceful and
successful period where hopes are realized and dreams come true.

SUGGESTIONS FOR:
LOVE: a fortuitous encounter or new relationship that is more rewarding than expected
WORK: a moment of glory, unwittingly received praise or improved image
HEALTH: surprise recovery, joy of living, no more health concerns

ADVICE: Be optimistic as things may turn out even better than expected.

LOCATION IN CROSS SPREAD:
- Above – Past: there has been an unexpected surprise or good luck recently
- Below – Future: the outcome is likely to be better than expected
- In front – Obstacle: action still needs to be taken in order to get the best outcome
- Behind: Advice: go ahead and do it, the outcome will be better than expected

REVERSED: This is not an overly negative card when reversed but it suggests a hope not realized or a positive event or outcome will be postponed. It doesn't mean that the outcome of the situation is negative, just that luck isn't on the inquirer's side or that they are facing a short period of bad luck. News may arrive late, there may be delays or an outcome will remain uncertain are all possible scenarios when this card appears reversed.

OTHER CARD SYSTEMS: Six of Clubs
- Vera Sibilla: Consoling surprise: positive and probably unexpected outcome, good for gambling and lottery, great results for little effort, positive financial card.

DATES: July 21 to 27

NUMBERS: 57 / 11

Sweetheart

Original Italian title: *L'Amante*, the lover, feminine

This is the female lover card. It represents the ideal lover or woman who is loved or loves.

- girlfriend, wife, lover, bride
- devotion, generosity, sensuality

SYMBOLS: The central figure of this card is a woman who is reading a note. She holds it close and her expression suggests that it is personal in nature. The abundant red roses and red cape symbolize passion and love. She leans on the red cape suggesting her love and passion steadies her. Her expression is relaxed and happy suggesting that the situation is positive and the contents of the note are pleasant.

STRAIGHT: The most common interpretation of this card is a person. If the inquirer is female, this card represents her, the person who is in love. When this card represents the inquirer, it suggests a positive answer to questions regarding love. It can represent a sweet and charming time for the relationship, suggests mutual love and affection and that the relationship is in a good place. It can also represent the woman that the inquirer loves or any loving, caring female, including a friend, wife, girlfriend, or sister. When associated with other "love" cards, this card may predict an upcoming wedding or engagement. Only when associated with very negative cards can this card suggest an ending, broken engagement, or breakup. This card can indicate that there is a potential rival or other woman if it is associated with cards suggesting deception or mystery. If this card is associated with the "Thief" card, it suggests that the inquirer should be cautious not to be deceived. If associated with the "Doctor" card, it suggests that the inquirer should reflect and possibly seek advice regarding the relationship.

SUGGESTIONS FOR:
> LOVE: this card is the woman in love, the other cards will reveal what to expect
> WORK: work relationships are harmonious or someone is providing support
> HEALTH: seek advice regarding gynecological problems, unlikely serious concerns, pregnancy

ADVICE: This is a time to trust your feelings and let go. Holding back could keep you from finding happiness.

LOCATION IN CROSS SPREAD:
- Above – Past: you have been in a loving relationship
- Below – Future: the relationship will blossom, a good period for love is on the horizon
- In front – Obstacle: potential rival love interest, or lover is impeding progress
- Behind: Advice: move forward confidently, feelings are mutual

REVERSED: This card reversed suggests unrequited love, disappointment or heartbreak. If the inquiry is whether a love will return, this card reversed suggests it is time to give up and move on. It can also suggest that the person the card represents comes from a broken place, which could be divorce, separation or a negative experience. This card can also represent a rival who is no longer in the picture. If this card is associated with positive cards, it may indicate that there is a chance for a recovery after an affair, breakup or disagreement. If the card is associated with negative cards, it could mean that the love has been lost and is unrecoverable. In work situations, this card reversed can suggest a complicated time when the inquirer may not be getting what she wants professionally and that it may be time to look for a new job.

OTHER CARD SYSTEMS: Queen of Hearts
- Vera Sibilla: Female Lover: a young woman, the inquirer, the inquirer's lover

DATES: February 4 to 10

NUMBERS: None

Thief

Original Italian title: *Ladro*, thief

This card represents a loss or someone who is coming to take what isn't theirs.

- sudden unexpected loss
- someone who cheats, steals or is meddling
- deception, betrayal, deceit, or damage

SYMBOLS: This card shows a man sneaking into a house through an open window. He is alone in the room but the house is definitely inhabited as there is a fresh flower in the vase on the table. The open window suggests the occupants have left the house unattended and vulnerable. The thief invades unexpectedly and takes away valuables that belong to someone else.

STRAIGHT: This is a negative card suggesting sudden or unexpected loss of property, love, time or work. This card warns that superficiality or inattention allows one to fall prey to the ill-intentioned. This card represents the wickedness, bad intentions, misdeeds, and bad thoughts of others that can rob us of our possessions, confidence, good faith or security. This card frequently suggests the presence of dishonest people who will take advantage of the situation when the inquirer's guard is down. If associated with other negative cards this card can suggest a significant loss, robbery, scam or fraud.

SUGGESTIONS FOR:
LOVE: the relationship is not working, one partner maybe living a parallel life, taking advantage, or betraying our trust
WORK: colleagues make secret agreements, working against or in bad faith, someone taking advantage of situation
HEALTH: small symptoms shouldn't be ignored, warning about more serious problems creeping in

ADVICE: Do not let your guard down or you could lose something important to you.

LOCATION IN CROSS SPREAD:
- Above – Past: something of value has been taken or lost
- Below – Future: there is a risk that something of value will be taken or lost
- In front – Obstacle: others will take advantage if they have the chance
- Behind: Advice: be vigilant, there are people who could take what is precious

REVERSED: This card continues to be negative when reversed because even in the presence of interruption or positive cards indicating the event is over, the effect of the dishonest actions, theft, robbery, or fraud has left a mark. If associated with document cards, it can suggest that there has been falsification of documents, or deliberately misleading information. This card always indicates that there has been misplaced confidence and that someone is taking advantage of the situation. Only when associated with very positive cards can the reverse indicate that there has been a narrow escape from the theft.

OTHER CARD SYSTEMS: Ten of Diamonds
- Vera Sibilla: Thief: Theft, everything that is taken away from us, something is fishy (especially in matters of the heart), economic problems

DATES: September 15 to 20

NUMBERS: 68 / 29

Thought

Original Italian title: *Pensiero*, thought

This card symbolizes thought, reflection and meditation.

- contemplation, introversion, reflection, indecision
- planning, decision making, judgment
- daydreams, visualization

SYMBOLS: The card depicts a mature man sitting at a table. His hand at his head suggesting he is deep in thought. He is likely an educated man and a scholar given the scrolled manuscript in one hand and the diploma on the table. On the table is a brazier with burring herbs, a skull and an hourglass. These symbols near him suggest that he is meditating. The burning herbs symbolize higher thoughts and connection to the spiritual. The hourglass is symbolic of time and that there is a set time for this contemplation.

STRAIGHT: This is a neutral card representing the need for thought, reflection, consideration and to tackle inner struggles. It suggests that the inquirer should take time to think before making any decisions regarding the situation at hand which could be a relationship, an intellectual challenge, an economic situation or a decision or judgment that must be made. This process could be quite difficult as there may be a lot of conflicting information to be analyzed. This card can also represent an idea or insight that comes from taking time for reflection. It can refer to a person who takes time to reflect before rendering a decision or insight. When associated with love cards, this could indicate the consideration of moving from friendship to love and the special thought this situation requires.

SUGGESTIONS FOR:
LOVE: need to find a way to resolve the situation, repair a relationship, move a relationship to the next level
WORK: new strategy needed to beat competition, careful analysis is needed to identify the right actions to take
HEALTH: follow doctor's orders, health is a precious gift, think things through and don't take risks

ADVICE: Take the time you need to carefully consider the entire situation before moving forward.

LOCATION IN CROSS SPREAD:
- Above – Past: something has been on your mind or under careful consideration
- Below – Future: the time is coming to carefully consider all aspects before making a plan or decision
- In front – Obstacle: a positive outcome will require contemplation and analysis
- Behind: Advice: take time to think

REVERSED: When this card appears reversed it suggests lack of thought, consideration or reflection or a person that acts in a thoughtless, impulsive way. This could suggest that the inquirer has not given a situation or decision enough thought or has given in to desires and passions without thinking through the consequences. This card is a warning to review what you are doing, to stop and think. It can also suggest a troubled mind, worry or anxiety that is not productive.

OTHER CARD SYSTEMS: Six of Diamonds
- Vera Sibilla: Six of Diamonds: Thought: the thoughts of the inquirer or someone else's, personality, use of mind, indecision

DATES: August 27 to 2I

NUMBERS: 72 / 33

Waiting

Original Italian title: *Belvedere*, lookout, viewpoint

This card symbolizes the sweet expectation of a pleasant event.

- waiting for someone, a specific event or answers
- yearning, hoping, wishing, wanderlust
- arrival of person, news, opportunity

SYMBOLS: This card shows a woman looking out over a city from a terrace. She he has a dreamy expression and appears to be happily anticipating the arrival of someone or something. The three red roses are symbolic of love and the number three symbolizes perfection.

STRAIGHT: This is a positive card symbolizing a time of waiting, anticipation or expectation for a person or event to arrive. The inquirer could be waiting for a loved one, wedding, engagement, news, message, a new job. This card suggests there will be a period of time that will need to pass before that which is anticipated will occur. However, this card suggests that once the waiting is over, the outcome will be positive. This type of expectation or waiting can be excruciating so this card can describe the emotions of anxiety, agitation and excitement associated with the wait. Only if the card is associated with negative cards could it suggest that the wait will be fruitless. For example, this card associated with "Letter" reversed could indicate that news or a correspondence that is expected will be delayed, not arrive or be negative.

SUGGESTIONS FOR:

LOVE: reconciliation, meetings with loved ones, anticipating the arrival of a new love interest or flirt

WORK: outcome of job interview will soon be known, news regarding estimates or proposals or payments will arrive soon

HEALTH: getting in shape will yield results, efforts are rewarded

ADVICE: Look to the future with confidence, don't give up hope, something good is coming.

LOCATION IN CROSS SPREAD:
- Above – Past: there has been a period of waiting for someone or something
- Below – Future: there will be period of waiting for someone or something to arrive
- In front – Obstacle: the challenge will be to be patient as there will be a time of waiting
- Behind: Advice: don't give up hope, anticipate good things are coming

REVERSED: This card reversed represents waiting unnecessarily, or disillusionment. As this card is an indicator of time, reversed it is a suggestion to stop waiting, that it is pointless or all hope is in vain. It suggests that an event will not occur or a person will not come. This could be that a loved one will not return, a meeting will not take place or there will be a rejection of an application or job. Particularly if it is associated with break or interruption cards, it indicates that the period of waiting has ended.

OTHER CARD SYSTEMS: Three of Hearts
- Vera Sibilla: Three of Hearts: Belvedere: arrival, waiting, something is on the way, some anxiety

DATES: June 3 to 8

NUMBERS: 76 / 34

Wedding

Original Italian title: *Imeneo*, hymeneal, of or concerning marriage

This card symbolizes partnership, marriage and commitment.
- important event, ceremony
- new responsibilities, contracts, unions
- loss of independence

SYMBOLS: This card depicts a wedding scene taking place in front of a domed structure that appears to be a church or temple. A couple exchange rings in the presence of a priest whose miter suggests he is of stature like a bishop or pope. The temple indicates the sacredness or the rite and the priest symbolizes the institutions and rules that are part of the ceremony. The groom is barefoot symbolizing virility and he holds a driving rod, suggesting he will be the one driving the couple.

STRAIGHT: This is positive card representing partnership, marriage, engagement, responsible love, the materialization of hope or the realization of an agreement or contract. There is an element of authority, law or destiny in the union. This card suggests a pivotal moment, one of decisive change or a significant new beginning or undertaking. In matters of love, it suggests true, sincere, approved and requited love. In other situations, it represents significant meetings or partnerships that are being forged.

SUGGESTIONS FOR:
LOVE: marriage, meetings between lovers, friends or family, new loving knowledge or love at first sight
WORK: business meetings, new professional negotiations, contracts being finalized
HEALTH: specialist consultation with very positive outcome

ADVICE: Enter into the marriage or partnership with confidence.

LOCATION IN CROSS SPREAD:
- Above – Past: a past marriage or partnership is a significant contributing factor
- Below – Future: there will be a marriage or partnership in the future
- In front – Obstacle: the challenge will be to come to an agreement and accept the new terms or arrangement
- Behind: Advice: the partnership will be a positive one, beneficial or satisfying

REVERSED: This card reversed suggests there is something that fate will not unite, an unrequited or impossible love, a canceled wedding or a broken engagement. This card can suggest a love that dies. This card can also suggest that the inquirer is refusing to accept the truth, that a relationship is ill-fated or a partnership or marriage is dissolving. This card can also indicate a clandestine romance, a love story without rhyme or reason or one that leads nowhere.

OTHER CARD SYSTEMS: Ace of Clubs
- Vera Sibilla: Ace of Clubs: Hymenaeus or Marriage: everything that is legally signed, partnership, marriage, sexuality, wealth, prosperity, conception

DATES: March 21 to 27

NUMBERS: 82 / 28

Widower

Original Italian title: *Vedovo*, widowed

This card symbolizes a person living with loneliness, sadness, loss or abandonment or the emotional state of mourning.

- mourning a loss, regrets
- need to accept a situation as over

SYMBOLS: This card shows an elegantly dressed man laying a wreath on a grave in a cemetery. He appears to be very sad and mourning the loss of a dear wife from the inscription on the headstone. The man is alone, symbolizing loneliness, solitary anguish and sadness. His elegant attire suggests his reverence, sincerity and continued devotion to the one who has been lost. The setting of a cemetery symbolizes finality, gone forever or a definitive loss.

STRAIGHT: This is a negative card in that it represents the feelings that come with a significant loss or separation. Whether it is the end of a love affair, loss of a job, a bad deal, the failure of a business, or loss of a friend or loved one, this card represents the feelings of sadness, loneliness and regret that can be suffocating. This card can represent a widowed person or someone who has not moved past the loss of someone or something. If the question pertains to a relationship, this card suggest that it is over and that the situation is difficult and complicated for the inquirer. This card also warns that one does not always appreciate the full value of something until it is lost. This card symbolizes the feelings of sincere and serious regret. This card also warns of a period of solitude and sadness that will be difficult to overcome.

SUGGESTIONS FOR:
LOVE: loneliness, widowhood, ruptured relationships, unable to deal with consequences of partner's actions
WORK: loss of job, economic losses, dealing with consequences of actions out of one's control
HEALTH: physical or mental suffering, accident

ADVICE: Acknowledge and accept that the loss is permanent and work to move on rather than dwelling on the past.

REVERSED: This card is more positive when reversed. If associated with positive cards it can signal the end of a period of solitude and sadness or at worst alternating periods of happiness and sadness. It can indicate that the time for mourning is past and it is now time to move on. When this card appears reversed with negative cards, it takes on a more ominous meaning of a sudden, irreparable, ending. It can be a love that ends abruptly that leads to despair and desperation.

LOCATION IN CROSS SPREAD:
- Above – Past: there has been a time of sorrow, loss or regret
- Below – Future: there will be a significant loss in the future
- In front – Obstacle: the challenge will be to deal with feelings of loss and regret
- Behind: Advice: accept the loss is permanent and work through feelings to move on

OTHER CARD SYSTEMS: Three of Spades
- Vera Sibilla: Three of Spades: Widower: loneliness, the ex, getting away from, loss, widower, bachelor, divorced man

DATES: July 3 to 8

NUMBERS: 48 / 36

Wife

Original Italian title: *Donna Sposata,* married woman

This card symbolizes a married woman, wife, mother, or ideal woman to start a family.
- trustworthy, loyal, honest
- caring, supportive, maternal, steadfast
- empathy, good judgment, understanding, gentleness
- committed relationship

SYMBOLS: This card shows a lovely woman with a child in her lap. The woman's expression is kind and relaxed. She holds a note, indicating she is informed and news is good. The child appears very well cared for suggesting she is a good mother, wise, responsible and mature. She wears a red rose, symbolizing she is loved. The setting is tranquil, a comfortable terrace with a beautiful view, suggesting prosperity, comfort and reassuring that life with this woman is good.

STRAIGHT: This card is a reassuring and positive card. This card represents someone who is generous, intellectual, confident and thoughtful. It also suggests someone of good moral character, one that is trustworthy and dependable. If the inquirer is hoping to be a wife, it suggests this wish will come true. It could also suggest that the inquirer has found the ideal person with whom to build a life and family. In business situations, this card represents someone who will help with the implementation of projects and one who will support prosperity and success.

SUGGESTIONS FOR:

LOVE: wife, mother, lover, friend that is reliable and sincere, good with children, loyal, sexually generous

WORK: co-worker or manager that is hardworking, talented and who drives profitability and growth of business

HEALTH: good health, strong passions, erotic energy

ADVICE: Trust that this is a person who is dependable and trustworthy.

LOCATION IN CROSS SPREAD:

- Above – Past: a dependable person has played a significant role in the recent past
- Below – Future: someone who can be trusted will play a role or will become a wife in the near future
- In front – Obstacle: the challenge will be to be loyal, supportive or to trust a female partner
- Behind: Advice: trust the person in your life to be trustworthy and loyal

REVERSED: This card reversed can represent a break, separation, or divorce. It can also describe a person who is not faithful, neglects responsibilities, is frivolous or lacking in moral character. It can suggest that the woman will not be a good and faithful wife or one with whom the inquirer should start a family. This card reversed also warns that projects could be delayed or canceled or there will be a disruption to the family. It can also represent a married lover or one that will break up the family.

OTHER CARD SYSTEMS: Queen of Diamonds
- Vera Sibilla: Queen of Diamonds: Married Woman: either a mature woman or woman who is in an established relationship, can be a mother

DATES: January 4 to 10

NUMBERS: 51 / 3

Young Woman

Original Italian title: *Giovinetta*, young girl

This card symbolizes a young woman or a situation that is young or still developing.
- damsel, daughter, sister, cousin, young lover
- sweet, reliable, polite, mannered
- maturing, growing, learning, developing

SYMBOLS: The central figure of this card is a young woman, no longer a girl but clearly young in years. She seems to be mature, demonstrating restraint and decorum. She is holding a book suggesting intellect, curiosity and desire to learn. In the background, there is a well-tended garden with a fountain. The fountain bursting upward symbolizes the life force and youthful strength. The garden is clean, tidy, healthy and green symbolizing the ability to mature and grow.

STRAIGHT: This card can represent either a person or a situation. When this card represents a person, it is a young female who is good, sensible and pure. When this card refers to a situation or entity it suggests that there is a need to grow or that an undertaking is premature. It can represent youthful enthusiasm, something undertaken with enthusiasm or a new venture that has yet to produce results. Associated with negative cards, this card can represent being restrained, confined, or having to grow up too fast.

SUGGESTIONS FOR:
LOVE: a pleasant flirtation is born and will perhaps mature into something mature and lasting
WORK: young employee or student, eager to learn, make a good impression, a first job
HEALTH: good health, female vitality

ADVICE: Give it time, things will mature and grow.

LOCATION IN CROSS SPREAD:
- Above – Past: something has been growing, maturing, coming of age
- Below – Future: there will be a period of growth in the future or a young female will enter the picture
- In front – Obstacle: the challenge will be to allow things to grow and mature
- Behind: Advice: allow time for growth and for things to mature

REVERSED: This card reversed suggests a lack of maturity, frivolity or something small and insignificant. It can indicate insecurity or something very young ending. When it refers to a person, reversed this card suggests a female who is listless, frail, lazy, unreliable or unambitious.

OTHER CARD SYSTEMS: Queen of Clubs
- Vera Sibilla: Queen of Clubs: Young Maiden: young woman or girl, sometimes inquirer, desire and waiting

DATES: December 4 to 10

NUMBERS: 81 / 20

Card Spreads

As discussed previously, Gypsy Oracle Cards are interpreted by the reader considering both the individual card meanings and the relationships between the cards that appear together in a reading. The groupings or layouts used for card readings are referred to as "spreads".

Reading with intention

Before laying out the cards into a spread it's important to set the intention for the reading. There are two aspects of this intention. The first is the intention of the card reader. You must be open to the energy of the inquirer, to set aside your own ego, bias and emotions to be able to discern what is important to convey. The second aspect of the intention is the question being asked and the spread being selected to answer this question. It is important to actively keep in mind all aspects of the intention as the cards are being shuffled. I have found that in order to have a clear picture of the intention, it's important to have the inquirer describe the situation or question being asked of me. Even if the inquiry is not very specific, setting a general intention to be able to convey what the inquirer needs to hear is perfectly acceptable.

Shuffling the cards

Whatever shuffle method allows you to thoroughly mix the cards mindful of the intention described above is fine. I have developed my own style that has been very effective for my readings. I begin by shuffling the cards at least seven times from my right to my left hand. I then set the deck face down on the table and cut it into three sections placing each cut to the left and allowing my intention to guide how thick each stack should be. I then rotate the middle section 180 degrees and then re-stack the deck in the reverse order (starting with the stack furthest right and putting it on top of the middle and then the combined deck on top of the stack to the left). I then reshuffle the deck seven more times from my right hand to my left. The rotation of a portion of the cards is important for my readings as I interpret the cards using both the straight and reversed orientations. The last step is to have the person making the inquiry cut the deck. I place the bottom of the cut on top and begin to deal the card spread starting with the top card.

Selecting which spread to use

There are many different spreads used by card readers. Some readers use only one type of spread for all their readings, while others, like myself, select the spread based on the type of question that is being asked or because I have a feeling which spread I should use in that moment.

In this section I will discuss several different card spreads starting with the cross spread that is described in the instructions that came with my Gypsy Oracle Deck and pictured below. I personally don't believe there are hard and fast rules about what spread should be used and why. What I do believe is important is that the card reader have a clear intention for the cards and which layout will be used. It is the reader who must tap into the energy of the inquirer and then interpret that energy with the aid of the cards, therefore, whatever spread the reader chooses with that intention will be the right one.

Cross Spread

```
              ┌──────────┐
              │    2     │
              │  Past    │
              │Influences│
              └──────────┘
┌──────────┐  ┌──────────┐  ┌──────────┐
│    5     │  │    1     │  │    4     │
│  Advice  │  │ Present  │  │Obstacles │
│          │  │Situation │  │          │
└──────────┘  └──────────┘  └──────────┘
              ┌──────────┐
              │    3     │
              │  Future  │
              │Influences│
              └──────────┘
```

Suggested Use

This spread is described in the leaflet that accompanies the Gypsy Oracle Cards. It can be used for all types of questions but is particularly useful for complex questions or situations where there are numerous possible influences and outcomes.

Dealing the Spread

Cards are dealt face down starting with the center card. Then a card is placed above, below, to the right and to the left of the center card. For a simple question, just one set of five cards may be sufficient but, for complex questions, the reader should deal four stacks. The reader then turns over the five cards on top and interprets the cards as a group.

Description of Card Positions

The center card (1) represents an aspect of the current situation. The card above (2) represents an element of the recent past that has contributed to the current situation represented by the center card. The card below (3) suggests how the situation will develop in the near future and represents elements that will influence the future. The card to the right (4) represents the obstacles or what is in front of or getting in the way of a positive outcome. The card to the left, or behind, (5) represents the advice, recommendations, suggestions or instructions for the inquirer in order to achieve their goals.

Interpretation

The cards are interpreted considering the meanings and locations of the cards. Take time to consider each card and how it relates back to the central card or present situation. Also, consider each group of 5 together and then at the end of the reading all the cards of a particular position. Predominantly negative or positive cards could suggest whether the answer is "yes" or "no". If there are common themes in the Advice or Obstacle positions this could suggest a pattern of behavior or strong recommendations that will influence the way the situation will develop.

Seven Card Spread

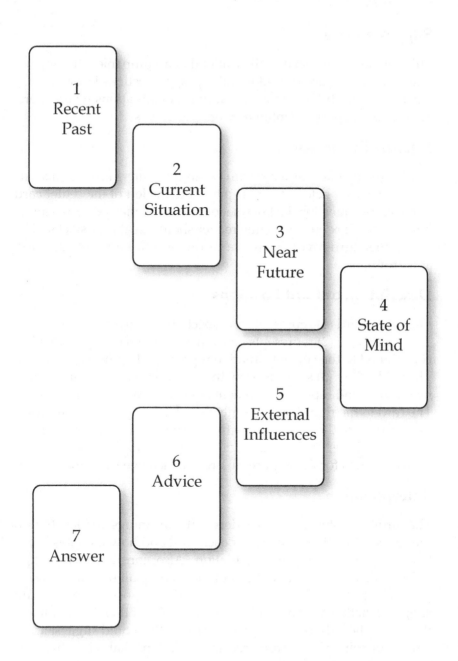

1
Recent
Past

2
Current
Situation

3
Near
Future

4
State of
Mind

5
External
Influences

6
Advice

7
Answer

Suggested Use

This spread is very useful for developing an answer to a specific question. This spread leads the reader to the answer while providing advice and insight into the factors that are influencing the situation.

Dealing the Spread

The reader deals seven cards face down from left to right and back in the pattern shown in the diagram to the left. All the cards are turned face up at once.

Description of Card Positions

The card at the top left of the spread (1) represents the most important aspects of the recent past. These elements of the past are ones that influence how the situation has or will develop. The next card (2) suggests the peculiarities of the current situation. The third card (3) reveals a peek at the answer and provides a suggestion for how the situation will evolve in the near future. The card furthest right in the middle of the spread (4) represents the emotions and concerns of the inquirer with regard to the question. The fifth card (5) represents the impact or influence of others on the outcome or answer. The next to last card (6) gives advice or recommendations for what actions should be taken. The final card (7) provides the answer to the question.

Interpretation

The reader should consider the meaning of each card in its position and discuss the card suggestions with the inquirer. By discussing the insights from each card, the reader can determine what aspects of the card meaning resonate with the inquirer . The story that emerges will help the reader build the interpretation of the spread and arrive at the answer to the inquiry.

119

Nine Card Spread

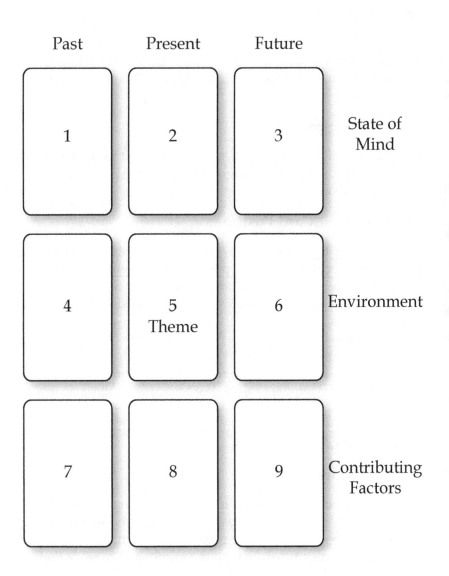

Suggested Use

Often the inquirer does not have a question in mind but instead asks for insights regarding a more general situation or aspect of life. For example, the inquirer could ask for insights regarding their career rather than a specific question about a work situation or problem. This spread is useful when there is no specific question but a need to understand the overall environment or theme for the next six to eight weeks.

Dealing the Spread

The reader deals nine cards face up in three rows beginning at the top left and moving from left to right as shown in the diagram.

Description of Card Positions

The center card (5) is the central theme or overall answer for the spread. This spread is most commonly interpreted by considering cards in groups of three. There are eight possible groupings to consider; three rows, three columns and two diagonal groups. The vertical columns represent the aspects of the Past (1,4,7), Present (2,5,8) and Future (2,6,9) that contribute to the overall theme or outcome. The top row (1,2,3) represents what is currently on the mind of the inquirer. The middle row (4,5,6) represents the present situation or the overall atmosphere surrounding the inquirer. The bottom row (7,8,9) represents aspects that are known and within the inquirer's control and suggest the actions that can be taken. The diagonal cards (1,5,9 and 3,5,7) provide insight into what other influences maybe at work.

Interpretation

Evaluate each row and column as a set to provide the interpretation for that aspect of the reading. It may be helpful to consider cards 2,4,5,6,8 together as they as they all represent aspects of the present situation. Also consider the number of negative and positive cards and their locations (in the past or future) and as an indicator of the direction the situation is headed.

Five and Three Card Spreads

Background Information   Overall Outcome

| 1 | 2 | 3
Central
Focus | 4 | 5 |

Past   Present   Future

| 1 | 2
Central
Focus | 3 |

Suggested Use

Five and three card spreads are useful for answering simple questions, particularly ones that are essentially "yes" or "no" and when the inquirer is not looking for depth as to the reasons why.

Dealing the Spread

After shuffling the cards thoroughly, either three or five cards are dealt face up from left to right.

Description of Card Positions

For both of these spreads, the card in the middle (card 3 in the five card spread and card 2 in the three card spread) represent the essence of the question being asked. For the five card spread, the two cards to the left (1, 2) describe the background for the answer such as the situations or people that are involved. The two cards to the right (4, 5) suggest the overall results from the situation. Similarly, the cards to the left and right in the three card spread represent the elements contributing to (1) and the results (3) for the question being asked.

Interpretation

The cards are interpreted considering the meanings and locations of the cards. Take time to consider each card and how it relates back to the central card or present situation. Consider the number of negative or positive cards in the spread. Predominantly negative cards suggest the answer is "no", whereas predominantly positive cards suggest the answer is "yes".

Relationship Spread

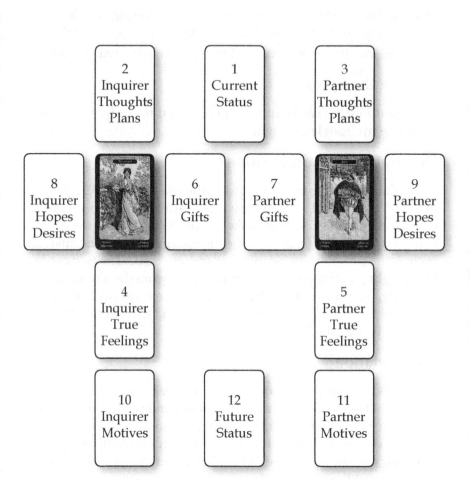

2 Inquirer Thoughts Plans

1 Current Status

3 Partner Thoughts Plans

8 Inquirer Hopes Desires

6 Inquirer Gifts

7 Partner Gifts

9 Partner Hopes Desires

4 Inquirer True Feelings

5 Partner True Feelings

10 Inquirer Motives

12 Future Status

11 Partner Motives

Suggested Use

As the name implies, this spread is useful for interpreting relationships. It is primarily used for romantic relationships but can be used for any type.

Dealing the Spread

Two cards are selected from the deck to represent the parties of the relationship. For romantic relationships it is customary to select the two lover cards (Sweetheart and Lover) no matter the gender of the parties, however, any two cards that the reader feels represents the people in question are acceptable. The character cards are placed face up on the table and the remaining cards are shuffled. The spread is dealt by first placing a card above and between the two character cards (1) and then dealing the cards around the character cards alternating between the inquirer and the partner in the order shown on the diagram.

Description of Card Positions

The first card (1) represents what is going on in the relationship at the present time. The cards above (2, 3) represent the person's thoughts and plans for the relationship. The cards immediately below (4, 5) represent what the person is really feeling about the other party and the relationship. The inside cards (6, 7) represent what each person is bringing to the relationship. The outside cards (8, 9) represent the persons hopes and desires for the relationship. The bottom cards (10, 11) represent what each person hopes to gain from the relationship and their motives for being connected the other. The last card (12) represents the future of the relationship.

Interpretation

Relationships are complex and interpreting this spread requires patience as there are many aspects to consider. It is important to consider the corresponding pairs of cards, such as the hopes and desires for the inquirer and partner (8, 9) and then the overall spread for each of the parties in order to evaluate the relationship.

Service of Reading

It is important to approach each reading with a genuine desire to be of service to the one making the inquiry. It doesn't matter if you are doing a reading for yourself or for someone else, nor does it matter whether or not you are monetarily compensated for your reading, you must focus on providing an honest and true reading. You must be mindful that you serve others best by delivering the insights that will help them navigate their situation, not what you want to say or what you think the inquirer wants to hear.

Each reader will have their own method for preparing themselves and their cards for a reading. For some it is very important to spend time meditating. For others it is performing a ritual such as clearing the energy of their cards and surroundings with crystals or incense. At a minimum, you should take time to focus on the service you are about to perform, and mindfully set an intention to see clearly the insights that will be most helpful to the inquirer.

I don't believe there are hard and fast rules for doing readings but, in general, my process is as follows:

1. **Quiet my mind:** I focus on letting go of my own thoughts, preoccupations and preconceived notions. I take a few deep breaths and open up my heart and mind to that which is beyond myself.

2. **Listen:** I ask the inquirer what they would like to know and then allow them time to describe their question, problem or situation. I shuffle the cards while listening, setting the intention that the right cards will appear to enable me to provide assistance. I ask clarifying questions to make sure I've understood the inquiry.

3. **Deal the spread:** After I've heard the inquiry I choose which spread I will use. I do a final shuffle and deal the cards with both the question and the spread I have chosen clearly pictured in my mind.

4. **Read the cards:** I take notice of which cards have appeared, evaluate their individual meanings, their position in the spread, and how they relate to each other. I allow myself time to take in the picture that the spread makes, the emotions it captures and the general feeling I get from the combination of words and images that have appeared.

5. **Speak from the heart:** I describe the cards and the picture that I see emerging to the inquirer. I may ask further questions to be able to be more specific in my reading.

Whatever process you choose will be the right one for you if it results in you being able to serve those who come to you with questions.

One final piece of advice; don't be afraid of negative or harsh cards. Be gentle in delivering difficult or unhappy messages, but do not avoid them as they may be just the right warning or advice that is needed in that moment. Trust that the cards have appeared for a reason and that their appearance is not a bad omen, rather guidance and support to help the inquirer face what challenges lie in their path.

Any reading conducted with an open and loving heart will be a good reading.

About the Author

Jacqueline is not easily defined. She is a scientist, business professional, photographer, musician, and now author with the release of her first book. Jacqueline's breadth of passions results from her curiosity, fearlessness and open mind which fuel her desire to experience new things, explore new places and be constantly learning.

From an early age Jacqueline had strong emotional responses to people and situations. She was encouraged by a dear friend to nurture and develop these instincts with the Gypsy Oracle Cards as a means to channel her intuition. Perhaps due to her Italian heritage, Jacqueline connected immediately with these cards. The desire to develop her intuitive gifts combined with her scientific approach lead Jacqueline to begin researching and documenting both her personal understanding of the cards along with the traditional meanings used by readers around the world, in particular, those in Italy where these cards have been used for generations. This work also lead to the realization that there were few good references in English for these cards and inspired Jacqueline to develop her folders of notes and research into this book.

Jacqueline has advanced degrees in both science and business and is fluent in several languages. She gains inspiration from travel and divides her time between her homes in the USA, Italy and Canada.

Made in the USA
Monee, IL
15 December 2024

73781508R00075